Thomas Francis Meagher as Captain of the 69th New York Militia's Company of "Irish Zouaves" (Company K) appeared in the <u>Irish American</u> on August 17, 1861. (Lt. Col. Kenneth H. Powers Collection)

THE IRISH BRIGADE
IN THE
CIVIL WAR

The 69th New York and Other Irish Regiments of the Army of the Potomac

69th Reg't N.Y.S. Vol.

JOSEPH G. BILBY

COMBINED PUBLISHING
Pennsylvania

Combined Publishing paperback edition, 1998.
Originally published in cloth edition under the title *Remember Fontenoy!* This edition is published by arrangement with Longstreet House, New Jersey.

For information, address:
COMBINED PUBLISHING
P.O. Box 307
Conshohocken, PA 19428

E-mail: combined@dca.net
Web: www.dca.net/combinedbooks
Orders: 1-800-418-6065

ISBN 0-938289-97-7
Cataloging-in-Publication Data available from the Library of Congress.

Printed in The United States of America.

CONTENTS

ILLUSTRATIONS

Note: The illustrations on the title page and on pages 144 and 269 are from patriotic envelopes in the Col. Kenneth H. Powers Collection.

MAPS

This book is dedicated to
the grandparents I never met
Joseph Geoghegan, (Co. Dublin) 1876-1938
Margaret McDermott Geoghegan, (Co. Leitrim) 1873-1941
and to
Maurice A. "Bud" Scully
who inspired me to write it

INTRODUCTION

It was, many said, the best brigade in the Army of the Potomac. Some said it was the best brigade in the whole Union army and perhaps the best brigade on either side in the American Civil War. Others, with the perspective of history, have come to believe it may have been the best infantry brigade that ever was.

It was Brigadier General Thomas Francis Meagher's Irish Brigade – the Second Brigade of the First Division of the II Army Corps of the Army of the Potomac. The II Corps' First Division lost more men killed in action than any other Federal division, and the Irish Brigade lost more men than any other brigade in that division.[1]

The unit which fathered the Irish Brigade, the 69th New York State Militia, established a reputation as a fine fighting outfit in a losing cause at Bull Run. Following the 69th's return from active duty the regiment provided a veteran cadre from which General Meagher built his brigade. The splendid organization created around this nucleus first met the enemy in the spring of 1862 at Fair Oaks, the II Corps' first fight, and served with the corps through to Appomattox Court House, its last.

William F. Fox, who knew the American Civil War's units perhaps better than anyone, wrote that the "Irish Brigade was, probably, the best known of any brigade organization, it having made an unusual reputation for dash and gallantry." The II Corps' historian, Francis A. Walker, pronounced the Irish Brigade "one of the most picturesque features of the Second Corps, whether in fight, on the march, or in camp." In its four year history, the brigade lost over 4,000 men, more than were ever in it at any one time, killed and wounded. The Irish Brigade's loss of 961 soldiers killed or mortally wounded in action was exceeded by only two other brigades in the Union army.[2]

Although the 29th Massachusetts Infantry and the 4th and 7th New York Heavy Artillery regiments were attached to the Irish Brigade at various intervals during its history, the brigade's core units were the 63rd, 69th and 88th New York Infantry, and, later, the 28th Massachusetts Infantry and the 116th Pennsylvania Infantry.

Strangely, except in the Fordham University Press' fine series of reprints, the details of the brigade's sterling record have been largely overlooked in the recent resurgence of interest in and new publications on the

Civil War. It is my hope that this book will convey at least a small part of the agony and the glory of the brigade's Irish American Iliad.

Through their bravery and steadfastness, the soldiers of the Irish Brigade did much to dispel the anti-Catholic, anti-immigrant phobias current in 1860s America. While prejudice would linger for several more generations, no one could accuse Thomas Francis Meagher's Irish American soldiers of a lack of loyalty to their adopted country. They had, in a way, fought and won two wars at once.

ACKNOWLEDGEMENTS

Portions of this book first appeared in the article "Remember Fontenoy," which appeared in *Military Images* magazine in 1983. I would like to take this opportunity to thank Harry Roach, editor of *Military Images*, for publishing the piece, which provided the genesis of this book.

Unfortunately, regimental tradition and loyalty have been largely lacking in the American army throughout its more than 200 years of existence. A happy exception to this sad record is the 69th New York, which remains an active unit of the New York National Guard. Whatever their own ethnic backgrounds, the 69th's current members and active Veterans' Corps constantly celebrate the regiment's proud heritage as a fighting Irish American outfit in the Civil War and World Wars I and II.

The 69th was the heart and soul of the Civil War Irish Brigade, and the regiment preserves the heritage of the entire brigade. The research material, illustrations and suggestions supplied by regimental historian Lieutenant Colonel Kenneth H. Powers, 69th New York Veteran Corps Commander Bernard Kelly and Veteran Corps member Michael Guirey were absolutely essential for the successful completion of this manuscript.

I would also like to take this opportunity to thank Dr. Anthony Collis, Dublin, Ireland, who provided me and my family with shelter and entertainment while I tracked down leads in the Irish National Archives, Mrs. Lucy Collis, who provided a fine Irish meal topped off with the best lemon meringue pie on either side of the Atlantic. Thanks are also due to Senator Joseph Doyle of the Dail Eireann, who generously interrupted his busy schedule to personally escort my visit to the 69th New York's second issue flag, presented to the people of Ireland by President John F. Kennedy in 1963.

On this side of the ocean, Brian Pohanka guided me to several invaluable sources, and my wife Patricia Bilby, Thomas and Janice Clancy, Ron Da Silva, Nick Ehlert, Jack Fitzpatrick, William C. Goble, Tony Hampton, Randy Hackenburg, James M. Heayn, Dick Johnson, Charlie Laverty, Joe Maghe, Michael McAfee, Ron McGovern, Jack McCormack, James Madden, Dr. David Martin, Charles B. Oellig, Steve O'Neil, Dr. Richard Sommers, Maurice A. "Bud" Scully Jr., Bill Styple, Michael Winey and Steven J. Wright provided research leads and material, illustrations, critical manuscript review and other vital assistance, without which this book would never have seen the light of day.

Last, but by no means least, the Civil War reenactors of Company A, 69th New York and the members of Company D, 69th New York, of the North-South Skirmish Association, provided vital and enthusiastic encouragement which helped this project come to pass.

Should I have forgotten anyone, I tender by sincere apology, Needless to say, any errors within are entirely my own.

THE
IRISH BRIGADE
IN THE
CIVIL WAR

NATIONAL CADETS.

HEAD QUARTERS, 69th REGIMENT, N. Y. S. M.

New York, *October 6th 1860*

W. B. Field Esqr.

Sir.

I beg to acknowledge the receipt of an Invitation to attend the Ball to be given in Honor of the Prince of Wales. As I am not desirous of joining in the Festivity it will be unnecessary for you to send me admission tickets.

Your Obt. Servant

Michael Corcoran

Colonel 69th Regiment

Letter of Colonel Corcoran refusing tickets to a ball in honor of the Prince of Wales, October 6, 1860. (Lt. Col. Kenneth H. Powers Collection)

Chapter 1

"Remember Ireland and Fontenoy"

I t was a matter of principle. It was not a question of insubordination or an example of ill discipline. At least that was the way the colonel and his men saw it. The colonel had, in the words of Thomas Francis Meagher, "refused lawfully as a citizen, courageously as a soldier, indignantly as an Irishman," to parade his regiment in honor of the visiting Prince of Wales.[3]

The colonel's regiment would not appear before the prince – and neither would he. On October 6, 1860, he declined an invitation to attend a ball thrown for the prince, informing those who invited him that since he was "not desirous of joining in the Festivity, it will be unnecessary for you to send me admission tickets."[4]

It wasn't the dissolute personal morality of the heir to the British throne to which the colonel objected. It was the little matter of the potato famine with its million unnamed dead. It was also the fate of "Young Ireland" in the abortive 1848 uprising and, beyond that, a whole catalog of ills and complaints, real and perceived, visited upon Erin by her neighbor across the Irish Sea. That was why Colonel Michael Corcoran refused to parade the 69th New York State Militia regiment for Queen Victoria's son.

There was no doubt his soldiers agreed with him. The 69th, originally New York State's 2nd Regiment of Irish Volunteers, was organized in 1851 from military companies founded by Irish immigrants who were either members of or sympathizers with the anti-British "Young Ireland" movement. In 1857, two other Hibernian outfits, the 9th and 75th New York Militia, were consolidated into the 69th. Irish militiamen of the 69th,

3

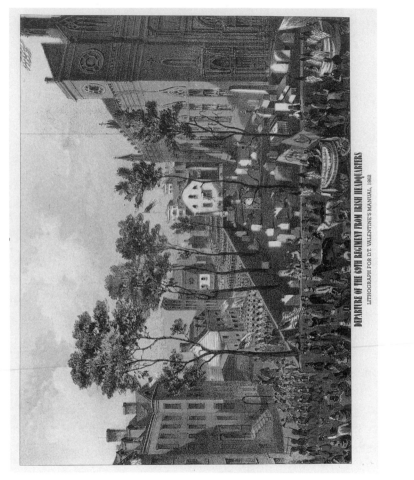

DEPARTURE OF THE 69TH REGIMENT FROM IRISH HEADQUARTERS

LITHOGRAPH FOR D.T. VALENTINE'S MANUAL, 1862

The 69th NYSM leaves for war in 1861. (Veteran Corps, 69th New York)

led by Corcoran, were among the founders of the Fenian Brotherhood, the American branch of the Irish Republican Brotherhood (IRB). The Fenians and the IRB were dedicated to the principle that an armed uprising was the only way to eliminate British domination of their homeland, and the Fenian foundations of the 69th were made abundantly clear during the Prince of Wales incident.

The state tried to court martial Corcoran. There was talk of disbanding the 69th, as Irish militia units had been dissolved in other states during the anti-Catholic "Know Nothing" hysteria of the 1850s. *Harper's Weekly* sourly referred to Irish militiamen as "not infrequently an absolute nuisance." Corcoran held firm.[5]

And then, on April 12, 1861, secessionist forces fired on Fort Sumter in Charleston harbor. Civil war had come, and with it the offer of the 69th's services to the Union. All was forgiven, the charges dismissed. Corcoran's regiment, only 245 strong, opened its ranks to recruits and, within days, mustered 1,040 Irish American volunteers for ninety days service. Some of the new men were no doubt Fenians, most were probably not.

On April 23, 1861, amid "deafening cheers" the 69th, the first Irish regiment to enter the service of the Union, marched from Great James Street down Broadway to Pier #4. The regiment's color party proudly bore a United States flag and an emerald color embroidered with a sunburst and red ribbons. The latter flag was presented to the 69th on March 16, 1861 by a group of Irish American citizens "In Commemoration of the 11th Oct. 1860," when Colonel Corcoran's regiment snubbed the Prince of Wales. The regiment was preceded to the docks by a four horse wagon bedecked with the motto "Sixty Ninth Remember Fontenoy." The banner recalled the triumph of the French General Maurice de Saxe over the British in 1745, a victory owed to an unstoppable bayonet charge by the French army's brigade of Irish exiles.[6]

The men of the 69th, many of them exiles in their own right, were soon on their way south aboard the steamer *James Adger*, and, after stopping to secure Annapolis for a brief period of time, proceeded to the capital. Arriving at Washington on May 4, the Irishmen set up camp at Georgetown College. With Virginia's ratification of secession on May 23, the 69th crossed the Potomac, occupied the critical terrain of Arlington Heights, and immediately went to work constructing "Fort Corcoran."

View from Fort Corcoran, with men of the 69th New York Militia, wearing Havelock head covers, in the middle distance. Beyond them is the Potomac River and, across it, Georgetown. (Anthony stereocard in Michael J. McAfee Collection)

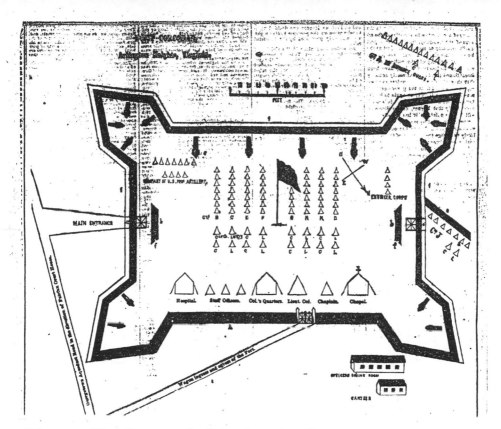

Diagram of Fort Corcoran, built by the 69th Militia in 1861. Woodcut from the *Irish American*, July 13, 1861.

The day the Irish crossed the river into Rebel territory, the regiment was joined by Captain Thomas F. Meagher's "Irish Zouaves," who became the 69th's Company K. Meagher's men were attired "most picturesquely" in blue jackets and vests, "those of the officers being heavily braided with gold, the non-commissioned officers' and privates' with crimson, the braids being worked into trefoils at the corners and intersections." Meagher's men wore pants of "regulation grey," with crimson and gold stripes and their kepis were adorned with "the number of the regiment in a wreath of shamrocks."[7]

Company K's commander was one of the most prominent Irishmen of his generation, at least on this side of the Atlantic. Young Ireland revolutionary, escaped political prisoner, newspaperman, orator and Irish and American patriot, Thomas Francis Meagher displayed a fire and enthusiasm for his native and adopted countries which would do much to rally otherwise reluctant Irishmen to the Union cause.

Father Thomas Mooney, Chaplain of the 69th Militia, celebrating mass in Virginia. Colonel Corcoran stands to Mooney's right. The Irish American for June 22, 1861 noted that "an employee of Brady the photographer" made this image (and no doubt others) on June 1, 1861. (Lt. Col. Kenneth H. Powers Collection)

After completing Fort Corcoran, the militiamen of the 69th built Fort Haggerty, named after the regiment's Captain James Haggerty. Haggerty, a smaller fortification, covered Fort Corcoran's flank as well as the Aqueduct Bridge to Washington. Father Thomas Mooney, the 69th's chaplain, caught up in the regiment's enthusiasm for its handiwork, baptized one of Fort Corcoran's cannon. When this sacrilege was publicized, the good father was recalled by his bishop and replaced by a Father O'Neil.

Mooney's transgression was overlooked by most newspapers, which were urging the Union forces gathering around Washington "on to Richmond." Most professional army officers realized that the green troops in Brigadier General Irwin McDowell's makeshift army were not prepared to undertake offensive operations. The ninety day enlistments of Union militiamen, including those of the 69th, were fast running out, however.

McDowell developed a plan to attack the Confederate force concentrated in the vicinity of Centreville, Virginia under the command of Brigadier General Pierre G. T. Beauregard before the bulk of his army evaporated before his eyes. The Union commander planned to advance with his force of 30,000 men against Beauregard's 20,000 while Major General Robert Patterson of the Pennsylvania militia, son of an Irish hero of the rising of 1798, threatened Brigadier General Joseph Johnston's force in the Shenandoah Valley to prevent Johnston from reinforcing Beauregard.

On July 12, Colonel Corcoran received orders to prepare his regiment to march with sixty rounds of ammunition and three days rations. Formal marching orders followed three days later. Confronted with the prospect of imminent conflict, the Irish militiamen of the 69th consoled themselves by confessing their sins or taking a sustaining sip of whiskey – or both.

Up early the next morning, the men of the 69th played the old and changeless army game of "hurry up and wait." Leaving behind Lieutenant Colonel Robert Nugent, injured in a fall from his horse, and Major John McKeon, commander of Fort Corcoran, the 69th joined the army's line of march at noon. Brigaded with the 13th and 79th New York and the 2nd Wisconsin in Colonel William T. Sherman's brigade of McDowell's First Division, the Irishmen marched to Falls Church, with the regiment's company of "intelligent, muscular, active and thoroughly hardened" engineers, each with "a reddish grey flannel blouse, and having a large for-

Colonel Michael J. Corcoran of the 69th New York Militia in a pre-war photo. Note crossed cannons on his hat, indicating the regiment's original role as heavy artillery in the forts of New York harbor. (Michael J. McAfee Collection)

est axe slung over his back," leading the way. Immediately behind the engineers marched the regiment's fife and drum corps, rattling and shrilling "old Dan Tuckerish" tunes. That evening the 69th halted near Falls Church and camped for the night in a marshy field.[8]

The following morning the Irishmen awoke cold and damp, then marched towards Fairfax Court House, with the engineers hacking their way through trees downed across the road by the retreating Rebels. They found the enemy at Fairfax, drawn up in line of battle. With muskets brightly burnished and cartridge boxes crammed with "buck and ball" ammunition, the Irishmen were spoiling for a fight and thought there was one in the offing. The Confederates withdrew, however, leaving behind a scattering of broken small arms and camp equipment.

Shortly after the Rebel retreat, the 69th suffered its first casualty. A loaded musket slipped off a stack of arms, hit the ground and fired, wounding Captain John Breslin of Company F. Instead of returning to Washington following first aid, Breslin was painfully jounced along in an ambulance in the regiment's rear, a situation for which Captain Meagher blamed "Colonel Sherman, a rude and envenomed martinet," who was "hated by the regiment."[9]

The 69th New York arrived at Centreville, along with the rest of McDowell's army, on July 18. The Union commander soon found the Confederates south of Centreville, on the high ground across a stream known as Bull Run. With Sherman's brigade playing a supporting role, other Union forces probed the Rebel defenses, looking for a place to ford the stream. At this point, McDowell outnumbered Beauregard. Had he attacked immediately, he may well have defeated the Southern forces.

As McDowell dithered, however, Rebel troops arrived by train from the Shenandoah, where Patterson had failed in his mission to occupy Johnston. Although the plan the Union general eventually arrived at was basically sound, he was unaware of the Rebel reinforcements when he launched his attack on the morning of July 21. The Yankees met with initial success, driving the enemy before them. As the morning, wore on, however, Rebel resistance stiffened and the progress of the offensive slowed.

When the 69th New York splashed across Bull Run and advanced on Henry House Hill to join the fight that afternoon, the battle was already several hours old. The midday heat was intense and many of the Irishmen discarded their uniform coats on the way up the hill. As

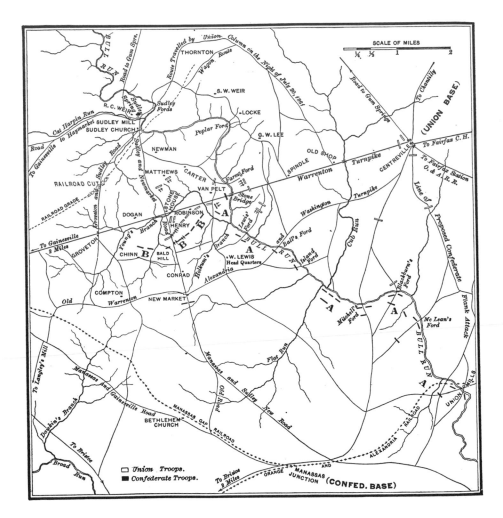

Battlefield of First Bull Run.

Corcoran's men neared the crest they saw some troops moving through the woods on their flank and prepared to fire. Quick thinking Captain Haggerty, the 69th's acting lieutenant colonel, rode along the regiment's line knocking up musket barrels with his sword, thus saving the Irishmen from firing on the gray garbed 13th New York. Tragedy avoided, the regiment laid down under bouncing cannon balls and bursting shells to await orders. One Irishman lost his ear to a shell fragment and was carried to the rear, where the 69th's surgeons welcomed him as their first patient.

As the Federal flanking force approached their position, the men of the 69th rose and advanced under sporadic artillery fire. The 4th Alabama, the last Rebel regiment left to their front, advanced towards the Irish New Yorkers, believing them to be fellow Confederates. As they closed on the 69th, the Alabamians waved their flag and received a close range volley of buckshot and balls in return. There are several unclear versions of what happened next, but when it was over, the Southerners, their colonel dead and lieutenant colonel and major badly wounded, fled. The fight was not entirely one sided, however. Captain Haggerty tried to ride down a running Rebel who turned and shot him dead out of his saddle. Despite Haggerty's death, victory seemed at hand as Sherman's brigade continued to advance.

Unfortunately for the 69th and the Union cause in general, the larger encounter did not reflect this local success. A Rebel counterattack swept over Union artillery which had been pushed forward without proper support, and Sherman threw his brigade in piecemeal in an attempt to recapture the guns. After the 2nd Wisconsin and 79th New York failed to retake the battery, the 69th was ordered forward. The Irish charged twice, clambering over the demoralized wreckage of the previous assaults – and were twice repulsed by a tide of small arms and artillery fire.

The arrival of more Confederate reinforcements, coupled with the exhaustion and disorganization of the attackers, led to the halt of a third Irish attack and the disintegration of the the Union army. The 69th New York remained an intact unit in the midst of the increasing chaos, however, withdrawing across the open fields towards Bull Run in a square formation, designed to repel cavalry attack. Unfortunately, as Colonel Corcoran changed formation from square to column to negotiate some difficult terrain, the 69th was overrun by two fleeing Union regiments.

Confederate cavalrymen firing carbines and revolvers suddenly

An artist's rendering of the 69th Militia in action at Bull Run. (*Leslie's Pictorial History*)

James McKay Rorty and Peter Kelly of the 69th Militia, captured at Bull Run, cross the Potomac River at the successful conclusion of their daring escape from a Confederate prison in Richmond. (*Leslie's Pictorial History*)

swept down on the disorganized mass of Yankees. Corcoran, who dis-mounted when his horse was wounded, waved the 69th's national color and attempted to rally his men but his "voice was drowned out amid the roar of the cavalry carbines and the discharge of artillery." The 69th, now swept along in the general rout, left Corcoran behind. Private James McKay Rorty of Company G blamed Colonel Sherman for the disaster. Accord-ing to Rorty, Sherman "told the men to get away as fast as they could as the enemy's cavalry were coming." Shortly afterward, Rorty and a num-ber of other Irishmen were captured along with Corcoran and the regiment's United States flag.[10]

The 69th's green banner was entrusted to the Zouaves of Company K, who were among the last Irishmen to leave the field. Swinging his sword over his head, Captain Meagher, the regiment's acting major, pointed to the Prince of Wales flag and shouted "Boys, look at that flag – think of

"The Return of the New York 69th Regiment, N.Y.S.N.G.." (Anthony stereocard in Michael J. McAfee Collection)

Ireland and Fontenoy." One Company K man later swore there was "not on this continent a braver man than Thomas Francis Meagher." Two color bearers were killed before the 69th's remaining color was ripped from its staff by a Rebel who was shot by John Keefe, one of the Zouaves. Keefe shot several other Confederates with his revolver in an unsuccessful attempt to retrieve the flag. It was, however, recaptured by Captain John Wildey of the New York Fire Zouaves and later returned to the regiment.[11]

Meagher's horse went down and he was knocked temporarily unconscious. He was saved from capture, however, when he was dragged to safety by a trooper of the 2nd United States Dragoons. Captain Meagher eventually hitched a ride on an artillery caisson, which pitched him into Bull Run when a horse was shot dead in its traces crossing the stream. Perhaps the last man of the 69th to leave the field at Bull Run, Thomas Meagher swam to the far bank and eventually rejoined the remains of his regiment, which staggered down the road to Fort Corcoran, arriving there at 3:00 AM the following morning. The 69th lost thirty-eight men killed, fifty-nine wounded and ninety-five missing in action at Bull Run. The New York Irishmen had acquitted themselves as well as, if not better than, any other Union outfit, regular, militia or volunteer, on the field.

Four days later, its enlistment expired, the 69th New York Militia went home, passing through Baltimore and Philadelphia to the cheers of an admiring public. Upon arriving in New York City, the regiment was escorted up Broadway by the city's militia companies, including the elite "Seventh Regiment with their white pants and bright gun barrels; several juvenile organizations in various styles of Zouave uniform," and a throng of civilian well wishers. A three gun battery fired a sixty-nine gun salute in the park across from City Hall. The uniforms of the bedraggled Irish veterans, who had lost much of their clothing at Bull Run, contrasted starkly with their resplendent escorts. One reporter noted that "every variety of undergarment was displayed under cross belts and knapsacks, and their caps varied from the fez of the Louisiana Zouave to the regulation hat (stolen by Floyd) of the Black cavalry."[12]

The Irishmen carried home other souvenirs from Virginia, including captured muskets, swords and revolvers. The most valuable trophy, however, was "...one of Sharpe's [sic] breech-loading rifles, with which the Black Horse Cavalry were armed," now the possession of Regimental Surgeon Barrow.[13]

17

Defenses of Washington, July, 1861.

"Broadway from Broome Street, Looking Up." A street scene in the New York City the men of the Irish Brigade knew. The photo probably dates from 1862. (Anthony stereocard in Michael J. McAfee Collection)

Although the men of the 69th New York Militia were released from active duty upon their return from Virginia, the interval would be a brief one for many. On August 29, 1861, Thomas F. Meagher made use of his considerable oratorical talents at a mass meeting in Jones' Wood to raise money for the 69th's widows and orphans. Along with its benevolent aspects, the rally served as a recruiting kickoff for the 69th New York Volunteer Infantry, which was enlisting volunteers for three years service. Several hundred veterans of the 69th Militia joined the new 69th. The old 69th retained its identity as a militia outfit for the remainder of the war, and beyond, but it was the regiment's offspring, the 69th New York Volunteers, which gained the fame and glory – and suffered the horrendous casualties – of the next four years.[14]

Offered the command of the new regiment, Captain Meagher never assumed the position, which was filled by Colonel Robert Nugent, former lieutenant colonel of the 69th Militia and now a regular army captain.

Although commissioned a colonel, Meagher had other fish to fry, chiefly the organization of an Irish Brigade, the cornerstone of which would be the new 69th. The words "Irish Brigade" were heavy with history and signified much more than simply a military unit composed of Irishmen to Thomas F. Meagher and his compatriots. Meagher's proposed brigade would assume the traditions of the famous expatriate outfits which once served France and Spain. In the new Irish Brigade, the spirit of Fontenoy would live once more.

Although many Irishmen were ambivalent about the war and their role in it, there was enthusiasm for the brigade among Irish American community leaders. The *Irish American* newspaper rhapsodized that "It [the brigade] is a splendid object, and one that may well excite the enthusiasm of Irish-Americans, with whom the name of Meagher is now, more than ever, a word of talismanic power."[15]

A recruiting station was established at #596 Broadway, and Irishmen began to come to the colors. Meagher informed one potential recruiter to "select none but intelligent, active, steady young men – men of decent character, and with a proper sense of the duties and dangers of the service." He intended his brigade to be an elite "legion" or combined arms outfit of two New York, one Philadelphia and one Boston infantry regiments, with integral cavalry and artillery battalions forming the brigade's fifth regiment. Although Meagher traveled to Philadelphia and Boston on recruiting missions, the governors of Pennsylvania and Massachusetts balked at sending recruits to New York, fearing their soldiers might be credited to that state. The 69th Pennsylvania and 28th Massachusetts Infantry would go to war as separate units. The brigade's cavalry unit never materialized at all, but four understrength artillery companies were mustered as the 2nd Battalion, New York Light Artillery, in December, 1861.[16]

The original Irish Brigade was thus an entirely New York state outfit of three infantry regiments, the 63rd, 69th and 88th New York, and the 2nd New York Artillery Battalion. The 63rd was already organizing when Meagher began to plan his brigade, but the 69th and 88th, largely officered by Bull Run veterans of the 69th Militia, were specifically designated for the outfit. Although all its units were credited to New York, and most recruits were from New York City, a significant number of the Irish Brigade's soldiers came from beyond the boundaries of Manhattan.

The first and last commanders of the Irish Brigade. Brigadier General Thomas Francis Meagher (seated) wears a uniform he designed himself. This may be the uniform he wore at Antietam, where W. L. D. O'Grady described the general as "gotten up most gorgeously...with a gold shoulder belt." The sword that General Meagher is wearing in this picture, a British Grenadier Guards Officer's pattern of 1854, was discovered in a deteriorated condition in a woodlot on the Wells River, Vermont dairy farm of Kenneth Alger on May 17, 1983. The 69th New York's regimental historian, Lieutenant Colonel Kenneth H. Powers, contacted Mr. Alger, who subsequently donated the sword to Meagher's old regiment. Restored at the Massachusetts Institute of Technology, the sword is now in the 69th's museum collection.

Brevet Brigadier General Robert Nugent (standing) has a plume in his kepi. It is probably the "green plume" described by Captain Turner in the pages of the *Irish American*. (Jack McCormack Collection)

The 69th's Company F was partly recruited in Brooklyn and many of Company K's men were from Buffalo. Company D came all the way from Chicago. Two companies of the 63rd traveled from Boston to join that regiment, while another came downstate from Albany. Most of the 88th's men enlisted in New York City, but Brooklyn contributed volunteers to Companies D and I and a number of Jersey City men joined Company G. The recruits for the 63rd assembled on David's Island in the East River while the 69th and 88th set up camp at Fort Schuyler, where a drill schedule alternated with family visits and fishing in the harbor.

The 69th New York was the first regiment to meet its minimum quota of men and was thus alternately designated the "First Regiment, Irish Brigade," which motto was embroidered on its regimental color. The banner, made by Tiffany and Company, was "a deep emerald green, to which the material, which is a heavy silk, imparts a rich sheen." The saffron fringed green flag featured a harp suspended between bright rays of sun descending from a cloud and a wreath of shamrocks. Underneath, on a crimson scroll, in Irish characters, was the motto, "Who never retreated from the clash of spears."[17]

The flag, along with a United States flag, was presented to the regiment in a November 18, 1861 ceremony at the Madison Avenue residence of Archbishop John Hughes, a fervid Unionist. Although the archbishop himself was in Europe on a mission for the Union, there was no shortage of clergy or laity on hand to praise the Irish Brigade volunteers. Judge Charles P. Daly delivered a stirring address which would have done justice to (and may have been written by) Thomas F. Meagher himself. The judge recalled a quote of Sir Charles Napier, who conquered an enemy army in India largely due to a "decisive charge with the bayonet" by a "thoroughly disciplined Irish regiment." Daly enjoined the 69th's recruits to emulate Napier's "magnificent Tipperary."[18]

The 88th New York, although not yet fully formed, also received colors that day. Mrs. Meagher personally presented the 88th's flags, which, along with the fact that the regiment was largely officered by Company K veterans, occasioned its nickname – "Mrs. Meagher's own." Because its number corresponded with that of a famed Irish regiment in the British army, the 88th was also known by that outfit's vernacular title, the "Connaught Rangers." The 63rd received its colors at its David's Island camp. Although the 69th was not at full strength, it was the only fully organized regiment in the brigade and so left for Washington immediately after the ceremony, 745 strong. The regiment was bid goodby by a throng which rivaled that assembled for the departure of the 69th Militia a few short months before. Reverend Matthew Hale, a Protestant minister with a growing respect for Catholics and their clergy, noted that there "were enough Irishmen on Broadway to have taken Charleston and Savannah combined, and women and children could not be counted for number."[19]

Although they received a splendid sendoff, the men of the 69th were less than splendidly armed by the state of New York, and carried 480 Prussian .69 caliber smoothbore muskets and 280 "long Enfield" rifle muskets to Virginia. While the soldiers armed with the British made Enfields had 2,000 rounds of ammunition to share among them, those unlucky enough to draw the smoothbores had to somehow divide a total of 150 cartridges.

The 88th and 63rd soon followed the 69th to Virginia. The two regiments, "twelve hundred men, under the green banner and wearing the green plume" left New York just before Christmas. They joined the 69th at "Camp California," on the Little River Turnpike, just west of Alexandria. The Irishmen were commanded by Colonel Nugent of the 69th until February, 1862, when Thomas F. Meagher, anticipating Congressional approval of his brigadier general's commission, arrived in Washington.[20]

Meagher had originally proposed former United States Senator James Shields, a personal friend of Abraham Lincoln, as the Irish Brigade's commander. Shields, who had served as a brigadier general in the Mexican War, was, at the outbreak of the Civil War, the most prominent Irish born soldier in America. When the brigade was formed, however, Shields was on a business trip to Mexico. When he finally returned the general expressed a desire for higher command and was offered a division. Although he lacked formal military education or training and had no combat experience save the Bull Run debacle, Meagher, whose inspiration gave birth to the brigade, was a logical second choice. Meagher's cause was not hurt when most of the brigade's officers petitioned Lincoln to appoint him to brigade command and Shields endorsed him as well. Perhaps more important was the official backing the brigade and Meagher received from New York Governor Edward D. Morgan.

General Meagher's official assumption of brigade command, which

General Meagher. (Michael J. McAfee Collection)

24

took place on a snow covered field at Camp California on February 5, inspired a rollicking impromptu celebration. Colonel Henry M. Baker of the 88th held an officers' party in his quarters, for which "Mrs. Baker and her sister, Miss Whitty, performed miracles in the culinary department." The assembled officers responded to Baker's toast of General Meagher with "three times three rousing cheers, ending with what Captain Hogan characteristically designates 'an Irish wolf dog.'" To light the night for the festivities, the brigade's enlisted men built a huge pyramid out of barrels purloined from Brigade Quartermaster Patrick Haverty and set them afire. A more formal, catered feast, with General Meagher and his officers serenaded by the band of the 2nd New Jersey Infantry, took place the following week.[21]

The celebrations were not universal. One anonymous correspondent, allegedly from the 69th, cast doubts on General Meagher's military abilities, citing the "general opinion of the regiment...that he is not" a capable commander. Colonel Thomas Enright of the 63rd also apparently opposed the appointment of Meagher, which was no doubt a determining factor in Enright's resignation the very day the new general assumed command.[22]

The men of the Irish Brigade spent the winter of 1861-1862 drilling and learning their role in the new Union Army of the Potomac organized under the tutelage of Major General George B. McClellan. In spite of his faults, which were many, McClellan was one of the most talented military organizers in the history of the United States army.

The "Young Napoleon's" army was composed of a kaleidoscope of Zouave regiments and ethnic units including the multi-national 39th New York "Garibaldi Guard" and the Highlanders of the 79th New York. The Irish Brigade took no back seat to any of these outfits, however, and its "Druid's Grove" headquarters at Camp California, dominated by the colorful Meagher, was decorated with the skin of a jaguar and other trophies the general had shot on a trip to Central America. After long days of drill, fourteen year old music prodigy Johnny O'Flaherty's violin and his father's bagpipes wafted the strains of mournful ballads of long lost rebellions against long dead kings through the cold night air past the general, who envisioned himself and his men as heirs to the traditions of which they sang.

On the whole, Meagher's men were healthy and well fed and

Irish Brigade chaplains and officers at Harrison's Landing, Virginia, prior to the brigade's departure for the Antietam campaign: seated l. to r.: unidentified officer, Rev. James Dillon, C.S.C., chaplain, 63rd New York, Rev. William Corby, C.S.C., chaplain 88th New York. Standing, l. to r. Rev. Patrick Dillon, C.S.C., of the University of Notre Dame (James Dillon's brother on a visit), James J. McCormick, Quartermaster, 63rd New York. (MASS/MOLLUS/USAMHI)

clothed. Extras arrived in packages from home as well, including "pieces of cake, a pair of socks, little et ceteras that only wives and mothers can and do think of; in many cases a small bottle filled with spirits which, under the circumstances, and considering the state of the weather, was...allowable even by the most censorious."[23]

Although Camp California, named in honor of the brigade's division commander, Brigadier General Edwin Vose Sumner, former commander of the Department of the Pacific, would be remembered with romantic nostalgia by some veterans, others would recall it as the center of a "dreary waste" plagued by severe winter weather. Lieutenant James B. Turner of Meagher's staff described a typical day in camp as "damp, dull, disagreeable; the rain is pouring, the sky is overcast and gloomy, the earth beneath your feet is a vast, treacherous, terrible sea of muddy matter, consisting of two-thirds clay and one-third water." Father William Corby, C. S. C., who left a comfortable position as a Notre Dame professor to serve as the 88th New York's chaplain, was shocked by the discomfort of winter soldiering. One morning the chaplain looked out of his tent and watched an officer crossing the street sink so deeply into the muck that he had to be shovelled out.[24]

The 88th's Father Corby, American born of an Irish father, the 63rd's Father James M. Dillon, C. S. C., and the 69th's Father Thomas Ouellet, a French Canadian Jesuit, devotedly served their military parish, mud or not. And a diverse pastorate it was. The personnel of the Irish Brigade ran the gamut of social class, with hod carriers serving alongside attorneys in the ranks. According to one account, some of the 88th's recruits enlisted shortly after they had exited the immigrant landing point at Castle Garden, and spoke no English, only the Irish Gaelic of the landless Catholic tenant farmer.

The preponderance of the brigade's rank and file were, however, urban workmen. Some of them were pretty tough customers. A soldier from Berdan's Sharpshooters reported that drunken stragglers from the 63rd New York being escorted to Virginia after the regiment's departure were so rowdy that some of their officers appeared afraid of them. In its initial months, the 63rd was something of a problem outfit, and a number of its officers, eventually including the colonel, resigned. In reality, however, most of the Irish Brigade's officers weren't afraid of anything on earth. They cultivated the image of the rural fox hunting "squireens" of the old country, a class in which physical bravery was, unfortunately, not always balanced by common sense.

A number of the brigade's officers and men had experience in a variety of military forces, including the United States regular army, the Papal army of Pius IX and the Irish regiments of the British army. William L. D. O'Grady of the 88th claimed that a third of that regiment's recruits had once taken the Queen's shilling. O'Grady himself, a former lieutenant in the Royal Marine Light Infantry, began his American army career as a private in the 88th.

Many of these veterans had experienced desperate combat and diverse life styles from Mexico, Italy, the Crimea to the Indian subcontinent. Captain Patrick T. Clooney of Waterford, who "went to Italy to fight for the Holy Father," in the Papal Brigade's Saint Patrick Battalion a year before he marched off to Bull Run in the 69th Militia's Company K, joined the 88th. The 88th's surgeon, Francis Reynolds, also an experienced soldier, served "on the British Medical Staff during the Crimean War." In a snow covered shack behind the brigade picket line that first winter of war, Reynolds introduced several officers to the dietary delights of food preparation in "scutari and Stamboul." The surgeon cut a steak into cubes, threaded the meat on a length of wire and broiled it over an open fire, producing, much to the delight of his companions, "kaybobs." Captain John J. "Jack" Gosson of the 69th was also, no doubt, familiar with eastern delicacies. Gosson had, at one time, soldiered in Syria, then served in "a Hungarian regiment, commanded by Prince Frederick Liechtenstein."[25]

Although some might characterize these well traveled Irish officers as "mercenaries," the term is singularly inappropriate. A mercenary fights for the highest bidder, no matter what the cause. There was no way a man like Patrick Clooney would fight for the Pope's enemies, nor those of the Union. Many Irishmen shared Thomas F. Meagher's view that the United States, which, despite occasional nativist outbursts, had welcomed Irish exiles and immigrants and given them economic and political opportunities they would never have had at home, was also the best hope to back eventual Irish freedom.

The collective military experience of these veterans of the Irish military diaspora played a major role in establishing the brigade's legendary fighting ability. Some of Meagher's men, were, however, veterans of less memorable military escapades. Lieutenant John J. Kavanaugh, who joined the 63rd New York in January, 1862, had been wounded in the thigh at the "battle of Mrs. McCormack's cabbage patch," in Balingary, the only action of the abortive Irish revolution of 1848, an affair which produced only one other casualty.

The men of the 69th would see a good deal more shooting in this war than anyone had seen in the McCormack cabbage patch. Many, especially the Fenians, were in this fight not only to assist their adopted country, but also because they viewed the war as good training for a future campaign back in Ireland.

Although the influence of the 69th militia was strongest in the 69th New York Volunteers, Colonel Corcoran's Fenians served throughout the brigade. Soon they would spread throughout the Union army. In November of 1861, the United States Navy precipitated an international incident by forcibly removing two Confedcrate diplomats, James M. Mason and John Slidell, from the British steamer *Trent.* The possibility of war between the United States and Britain provided a strong stimulus to Fenian enlistment in the Union army, and some fifty Fenian "circles" or branches ceased to exist when all their members donned the blue. The "Bold Fenian Men" of the Irish Brigade and a number of other Civil War units, Union and Confederate, would nurture a patriotic fire in their breasts through four hard years of war. Some of the survivors would try, once more unsuccessfully, to raise the flag of rebellion over the "four green fields."

It is not clear that all the soldiers in the 69th New York and the other regiments of the brigade had such a mission in mind, however. Dr. Lawrence Kohl's survey of 500 Irish Brigade enlistment records in the New York State Archives indicated that "the great majority of the men of the brigade were married, older men who had already taken out American citizenship." According to Kohl: "These were hardly the type who would have been most likely to have rushed back to Ireland to fight against the British." While Fenian enthusiasm was certainly high among the politically active militiamen of the pre-war 69th who refused to parade for Queen Victoria's "Bertie," there may well have been less activism among the post Bull Run recruits of the 63rd, 69th and 88th New York Infantry.[26]

There is evidence that emotional ties to Ireland and its troubles remained strong, even among Irish Brigade soldiers born on this side of the Atlantic. As in most human endeavors, however, enlistment motivations were often mixed. In a letter to his father-in-law in Ireland, thirty-two year old Canadian born Peter Welsh of the 28th Massachusetts (which joined the Irish Brigade following the battle of Antietam) hoped that he "might one day...strike a blow for the rights and liberty of Ireland." Although Welsh's deep conviction in the correctness of the Union cause is also evident in his letters, he declined the opportunity to enlist in the Irish Brigade in 1861, even though he was living in New York and a good friend joined the 88th. The immediate motivation for Welsh's enlistment in the late summer of 1862 was a visit to Boston in which he "got on the spree and spent all the mony i had with me..." Welsh's "shame and remorse" and fear of confronting wife and friends after his binge led him to the recruiting office.[27]

Other men, especially older ones, no doubt came to the colors out of economic necessity. The outbreak of war spawned economic dislocation and depression which, while it would eventually abate, was deep and real for the first year of the conflict. Irish immigration declined measurably in 1861 and one Ulsterman in the United States reported that "the times is miserable in this countrey..." A Boston Irishman wrote that "all the people who have lived by their labour and only from hand to mouth...are going to the war." At the same time, poor harvests in Ireland left few with the money to buy a ticket to America.[28]

Even Fenian activists had mixed motivations for joining the army. James McKay Rorty, along with fellow Bull Run POWs First Sergeant William O'Donohue and Private Peter Kelly of the 69th Militia, succeeded in a daring escape from a Rebel prison in Richmond and successfully reached Union lines. Rorty was subsequently commissioned a second lieutenant in the 2nd New York Artillery Battalion's Company D. In a letter to his disapproving parents, Rorty cited the "gloomy appearance of business" and the potential to eventually use his military skills "in the sacred cause of my native land," as reasons for reenlisting. Perhaps as important, he liked the military life. Rorty had joined the 69th Militia "a shy, morose, and gloomy being, weak in body and with fluctuating health...," but had acquired "a cool, steady self possession" during his brief period of service. In short, whatever it had done for or to others, the 69th's fight at Bull Run had made James McKay Rorty a man.[29]

Chapter 2

"Like Brothers in a Fight"

For James McKay Rorty and his fellow Fenians, military efforts in "the sacred cause" lay in a future dimly perceived, and there was work to do now for the Union. Abraham Lincoln wanted the work to begin as soon as possible, and ordered all Union armies to assume the offensive on February 22, 1862. Although General McClellan didn't comply, the order stimulated him to reveal his plan to outflank the Confederates in Virginia through an amphibious operation. The Federal commander was forced to modify his plan when General Joseph Johnston withdrew his army from the Manassas line he had held all winter.

Union forces, among them General Meagher's Irish Brigade, moved forward to confirm Johnston's withdrawal. In late March the Irishmen sloshed down muddy roads and crossed swollen streams in an advance on the abandoned Rebel camps at Manassas. At one point Father Corby's horse, a quartermaster nag, stopped in midstream and had to be prodded with a bayonet to get the chaplain to the other bank. The Irishmen of the 69th's Company B, under Captain Thomas Leddy, got a brief glimpse of the enemy at Warrenton Junction. Company B skirmished with retreating Rebel cavalry, but incurred no losses.

After returning to Camp California wet, tired and hungry, the Irishmen boarded the steamer *Ocean Queen* and the *Columbia*, "an East River ferry-boat, with a new floor in the roadway, the officers being in the cabins, and the men in the roadway." When the transports entered Chesapeake Bay, the *Columbia* "began to ship water and finally a wave of solid volume came over the bow," soaking the Irishmen to the skin.[1]

General McClellan's new plan called for a landing on the Virginia

31

Maurice A. Scully Jr., Company D, 69th New York, North-South Skirmish Association, with a U. S. Model 1816 smoothbore .69 caliber musket converted from flintlock to percussion ignition. General Meagher preferred smoothbore arms such as this for his men, depending on lethal close range "buck and ball" rounds followed by a bayonet charge to secure victory. Scully wears a reproduction of the New York "state coat" issued to New York soldiers in the first years of the war. (Joseph Bilby)

Peninsula, situated between the James and York Rivers, within easy striking distance of Richmond and behind Johnston's main Rebel army, now deployed on the Rappahannock River line. McClellan had outgeneraled Johnston, but would, unfortunately, outgeneral himself in the months to come.

The Union army sailed to the Peninsula with a new table of organization. Without consulting the troublesome McClellan, Secretary of War Edwin M. Stanton assigned the Army of the Potomac's divisions to four new army corps in March. General Sumner assumed command of the II Army Corps, and the Irish Brigade became the Second Brigade of Brigadier General Israel B. "Fighting Dick" Richardson's First Division of the corps. By contemporary standards the brigade was well prepared for action. It was seasoned with veteran officers and men, thoroughly drilled in *Hardee's Tactics* and had been uniformly reequipped with U. S. .69 caliber smoothbore muskets.

General Meagher probably could have secured more modern .58 caliber rifle muskets or imported guns of the same style, which provided greater long range accuracy, for at least some of his men. He specifically requested .69 caliber smoothbores, however. Although these guns were deemed obsolete by many, Meagher felt that smoothbores loaded with "buck and ball" were the most effective weapons available for the close fighting he envisioned for his Irishmen. The general believed a volley of buckshot and balls, followed by a bayonet charge, would carry the day, as at Fontenoy. He viewed Irish impetuosity and elan coupled with cold steel as incalculable military advantages that would consistently deliver victory. Meagher's theory, part of the burden of Irish military history, became brigade doctrine, and would gain the Irishmen great renown – and heavy losses – in the months ahead.[2]

For the moment, at least, the soldiers of the Irish Brigade were enthusiastic for the coming fight. Not all of them were men. "Big Mary," Gordon, a "cantiniere" in the European tradition, accompanied the 88th to the Peninsula. Mrs. Gordon was "one of the jolliest and handsomest of young Irishwomen...whose little husband minded the colonel's famous horse 'Faugh a Ballagh' while she washed his shirts and those of several officers whom she favored."[3]

The 2nd New York Artillery Battalion would not accompany the brigade's three infantry regiments to the Virginia Peninsula as an independent organization. Understrength and riven with internal disputes and court martials, the battalion was broken up and its guns and men assigned to Battery C, 4th U. S. Artillery, and Batteries B and C, 1st New York Artillery Battalion. These detached sections were later reclassified on paper as the 14th New York Independent Battery, but continued to serve with the batteries they were assigned to. On the Peninsula, all of these batteries remained assigned to General Richardson's division, the Irish Brigade's parent organization.

While Meagher's men sailed south along the Virginia coast, Captain Theodore Kelly and Lieutenants James M. Canton and John Fahy of the 69th Militia moved overland through the state to Cub Run, near Manassas, where the body of Captain James Haggerty had been hastily buried by his men the previous July. With some difficulty the officers disinterred Captain Haggerty's decomposed remains and returned them to New York for reburial. Mrs. Haggerty insisted that her husband's lead lined mahogany coffin be opened, "and was overcome with grief." But the 69th did not forget its heros.[4]

Haggerty's former comrades in the Irish Brigade were not given an early opportunity to demonstrate their own courage in combat that April. Bluffed by an inferior Confederate force under Major General John B. Magruder at Yorktown, McClellan deployed his army for a siege. The Irishmen were initially assigned to dig gun emplacements and "corduroy" muddy roads with logs. It may have been war, but, as yet, it wasn't hell. Although the men of the brigade were subjected to sporadic artillery and sniper fire, the 69th's first casualty was accidental. Private Patrick Casey of the regiment's company B was killed when a tree fell on him.

As the siege lengthened, the living conditions of the besiegers grew more comfortable. The Irish Brigade "encamped in the most delightful manner possible." James B. Turner, now a captain, informed the readers of the *Irish American* that "many tents have between them ornaments and devices of various kinds, harps and shamrocks preponderating." Company streets were decorated on either end with arches woven from evergreens.

As McClellan's host grew, General Johnston withdrew the bulk of his forces from the Rappahannock line, assumed overall command of Confederate forces defending Richmond and decided to evacuate Yorktown. When the Rebels suddenly decamped and retreated towards

Richmond on May 3, the Irish Brigade left its cozy camp behind to join the Army of the Potomac's pursuit. The Irishmen slogged through swamps and along muddy roads up the Peninsula towards the enemy capital. The Rebels turned on their pursuers at Williamsburg on May 5, and, following a vicious rear guard battle in the rain, continued their retreat towards Richmond.

The Irish Brigade arrived at Williamsburg after the fight, then turned around, marched back to Yorktown, boarded ships and sailed to West Point on the York River. An officer of the 63rd later recalled an officer's wife who accompanied the brigade on this series of moves, with an "immense green feather in her hat and dark green riding habit attracting no little attention." The rigors of campaigning quickly left the lady in a bedraggled state, however, and she soon returned to New York.[5]

The steady, if slow, advance of the Army of the Potomac on his capital during the following weeks made President Jefferson Davis increasingly nervous. With the Federals closing in on Richmond, Joseph Johnston, as cautious a man as McClellan, was pressed to take the offensive. Johnston decided to attack Brigadier General Erasmus D. Keyes' isolated IV Corps, deployed south of the Chickahominy River, which bisected the Peninsula. The IV Corps' Second Division held the corps' front at the intersection of the Williamsburg and Nine Mile Roads, and picketed a line between Seven Pines and the Fair Oaks Station of the Richmond Railroad. The IV Corps' First Division was deployed to the Second's rear.

In the wake of heavy spring rains the Chickahominy swelled almost to flood stage. The rising river threatened the rickety bridges over which reinforcements for Keyes' men would have to march, increasing the IV Corps' vulnerability. Realizing this, McClellan moved the III Corps, under Major General Samuel P. Heintzelman, across the Chickahominy. Heintzelman assumed operational control of both corps, although his own unit remained several miles to the rear of the IV Corps.

Deploying the divisions of Major Generals Ambrose P. Hill and John B. Magruder to hold the line north of the Chickahominy, General Johnston directed forces under the command of Major Generals James Longstreet and Daniel H. Hill to attack the IV Corps. Major General Gustavus W. Smith was instructed to support the attack with his division while Major General Benjamin Huger was ordered to move his division

Soldiers completing work on the Grapevine Bridge across the Chickahominy, May 29, 1862. The work party has been identified as soldiers of the 5th New Hampshire, 64th New York and the Irish Brigade. Some of these men appear to be wearing the short New York "state" coats. The Irish Brigade crossed this bridge on its way to Fair Oaks on the night of May 31, 1862, with the river almost at flood stage. (MASS/MOLLUS/USAMHI)

down the Charles City Road to protect the Confederate right as well as threaten the Union rear. At least that seems to have been the plan. Johnston's orders were verbal rather than written, and, in the months and years after the battle, none of the principle participants could agree on what they were. In the event, Longstreet apparently got his men on the wrong road, blocking the advance of Huger. What was supposed to be a surprise dawn attack on May 31 didn't get underway until afternoon. Although late, the attack was effective, and the Confederate onslaught hit the Yankees along the Seven Pines/Fair Oaks line like a sledgehammer, virtually wrecking the IV Corps.

General Heintzelman's III Corps advanced through beaten Yankees streaming to the rear, stabilized the front and eventually halted the Confederate pursuit. The Rebels' partial victory that day cost them dearly, however, and General Johnston himself was among the wounded. Elements of the II Corps, which were deployed north of the Chickahominy, were ordered to cross the river to assist the beleaguered III and IV Corps men in the vicinity of Fair Oaks Station.

As Johnston's army began its attack at Seven Pines, the Irish Brigade's officers were busy conducting the "Chickahominy Steeple Chase." Father Corby and other American born soldiers had never seen a steeple chase, which was "unquestionably...the invention of wild Irishmen, who did not know what fear is!"

As "the little major" James Cavanagh of the 69th successfully leaped ditches and brushpiles and came in a winner astride "Katie Darling," the brigade received orders to cross the Chickahominy.[6]

The Irish Brigade marched to the river "in the lightest possible marching order, the men taking with them in their haversacks only two days' cooked rations, and being disencumbered of their overcoats, knapsacks and blankets." Diverted from their intended crossing point, the Lower Bridge, which was falling apart, the Irishmen sloshed through mud and floating corduroy logs to the Grapevine Bridge, where they followed Brigadier General John Sedgewick's brigade across that rickety structure as the swelled Chickahominy, distressingly alive with struggling snakes, swept under and around their feet. Leaving the 63rd behind to guard the bridge, General Meagher led the 69th and 88th forward on a spongy path into the "dark, dismal swamps of the Chickahominy."[7]

The exhausted Irishmen marched on into a black hole of a night

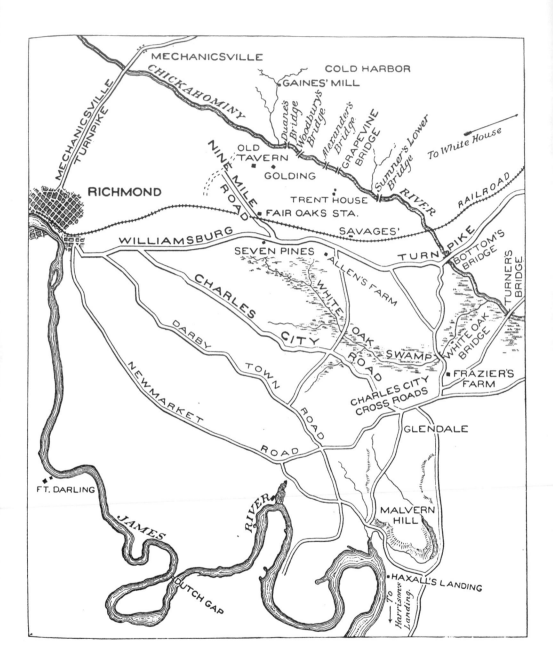

Richmond and vicinity.

until flickering lanterns signalled soldiers seeking the wounded and sporadic musket shots from the picket line warned that the enemy was close at hand. The men of the 69th and 88th collapsed into sleep in an open field around 9:00 PM, only to rise and form ranks at 4:00 AM. As the sun rose over the field, the Irishmen found themselves in the midst of a jumble of broken muskets, looted knapsacks, overturned artillery, an abandoned, blood soaked ambulance and the swelling corpses of the previous day's dead.

While the men of the 63rd pulled the First Division's artillery out of shoe sucking swamp mud, the 69th and 88th deployed to fill a reserve position on the Fair Oaks line between Brigadier General Philip Kearny's III Corps division and other elements of the II Corps. One athletic Irishman from the 69th, "an immense, shaggy iron built fellow, with a tanned skin and a tempestuous eye, agile and daring as a tiger," shinnied up a tree for a look-see at the spires of Richmond, several miles away.[8]

As muskets popped in the woods to the front, General Sumner rode up to the Irish and ordered them, along with the Yankees of the 5th New Hampshire, forward to replace Union regiments driven back by a Rebel advance. Battle came first to the 69th, which moved in column alongside the Richmond Railroad. As the regiment closed on the woods to its front it came under enemy fire, and Private Michael Herbert of Company I, a veteran of the Sepoy Rebellion in India and service with the Papal Brigade in Italy, fell mortally wounded. Unfazed as men dropped, the soldiers of the 69th deployed into line and blazed away, trading volley for volley until the Rebel fire slackened and then stopped. Captain Felix Duffy, who joined the firefight, got a bit of a range advantage on his boys by arming himself with a rifle musket.

Shortly after the 69th advanced, Lieutenant Colonel Patrick Kelly led the 88th, in line of battle, into a "tangled underwood, encumbered with fallen and decayed trees, interspersed with heavy patches of mire and swamp." After struggling through the woodlot, Kelly emerged into an open field with only two companies. Under small arms fire, as well as a stinging attack by a force of Confederate bees, the lieutenant colonel led his impromptu battalion in a charge across the field, seized a good defensive position and held off the Rebels until the regiment's other eight companies joined him.[9]

Reunited, the boys of "Mrs. Meagher's Own" took a position in a gully which afforded them some cover and a flanking angle on the Rebels, who soon broke for the rear. Young Musician George Funk of the 88th forsook his drum for a musket, slipped out to the skirmish line and captured a Grayback soldier twice his size. Senior Federal commanders were delighted with the Irish Brigade's aggressive behavior. One Irish officer reported that "Gen. Sumner said that if an Irishman ran he would run himself, and when Gen. McClellan rode up he gave particular praise to the Irish Brigade." Another soldier boasted that "the splendid vollies of the brigade [69th and 88th] were conspicuous and effective.[10]

During the battle Father Corby rode with General Meagher and his staff, a short distance behind the battle line. Although somewhat unnerved by bullets whizzing above his head, the priest kept up with the other officers. At one point he dismounted to pray with a dying soldier propped up against an abandoned log cabin. The chaplain administered the last rites to the accompaniment of bullets bouncing like hailstones off the cabin roof.

Following the fight, sixteen year old Private Peter Rafferty of the 69th's Company B set out with a comrade on a souvenir hunt. Passing a dead enemy soldier whose torso was submerged in a bog while his feet stuck up in the air, the Irishmen made a note to return for the Rebel's "fine pair of leather boots." After crossing a creek and climbing a hill, Rafferty and his companion found a field full of wounded and dead Rebels and a barrel of whiskey stored in a nearby barn.[11]

Laden down with five canteens of whiskey each, and pipes and Confederate money lifted from the dead, the two Irish Yankees headed back to their regiment. On the way they met Father Ouellet, who requested some of their "water" for the wounded. Surrendering a canteen of whiskey each to the chaplain, Rafferty and his friend returned to the bogbound Rebel. They were too late; someone had relieved the dead man of his boots.

In the aftermath of Fair Oaks, the Irish Brigade was reinforced by the addition of the 29th Massachusetts Infantry. Although a "Yankee" unit largely composed of native born American Protestants, the 29th was welcomed by General Meagher and the brigade. The Irish Brigade, with the rest of the II Corps, remained south of the Chickahominy. In a reverse of the tactical situation existing before the battle, the majority of McClellan's forces were now south of the river.

The Irishmen dug in, strengthening their position, which was close by a mass grave filled with the dead of Fair Oaks. As the month of June wore on, soldiers from the 69th saw wraiths rise in the night "over the trench of the dead." Some saw images of "soldiers known and unknown," others "women and weeping children," who, "after a few moments would pass away, and others would form and vanish the same way." Not everyone, including those who had proved themselves in battle, had the nerve to peek over the trench berm at these shimmering souls, which, no doubt, grew out of "will o' the wisp" marsh gases and overactive imaginations. Perhaps.[12]

While the Irish settled into their new positions, they were visited by Spanish General Juan Prim. When Prim queried: "What troops are these?" and was informed they were the Irish Brigade, he recalled the Spanish army's Irish Brigade, noting that "Spain has reason to appreciate Irish valor. Spain and Ireland were allies from ancient times and stood shoulder to shoulder on many a well fought field." A translation of the general's words drew a hearty cheer from the assembled Irishmen. As he rode away, Prim quipped: "I don't wonder the Irish fight so well; their cheers are as good as the bullets of other men."[13]

One unfortunate effect of Fair Oaks for the Federals was the replacement of the wounded General Johnston by General Robert E. Lee, a much more aggressive adversary who astutely surveyed the Federal dispositions. Major General Fitz John Porter's V Corps remained north of the Chickahominy, where McClellan hoped Porter would would make contact with General McDowell's Corps, which was tentatively moving south by the overland route.

The Yankees would never meet. McDowell's men were diverted when Confederate Major General Thomas J. "Stonewall" Jackson's Shenandoah Valley campaign threatened Washington. While McDowell delayed, General Lee decided to concentrate his own forces, including Jackson's fast moving "foot cavalry," and attack the isolated Porter in order to drive the Union army from the suburbs of Richmond. As Porter fell back fighting on Gaines' Mill in late June, McClellan, suffering from the perpetual fantasy that he was outnumbered, made a decision to change his supply base by withdrawing his entire army to the James River. While McClellan made up his mind, the Irish Brigade skirmished constantly on the picket lines. The brigade was constantly on the alert, and one officer noted that "the enemy's pickets (their sharpshooters) can throw their rifle

41

balls right into our camp." On June 18, the Irishmen took part in a reconnaissance in force which drove in the enemy's picket line and gave them temporary relief.[14]

"Mac's" decision to pull the V Corps back across the Chickahominy came too late for Porter's men. On June 27, 1862, reinforced by Jackson's Valley soldiers, Lee launched an all out assault on the V Corps position at Gaines' Mill. Although reinforced by Brigadier General Henry W. Slocum's First Division of the VI Corps, Porter's position was overrun late in the afternoon.

The Irish Brigade, then camped at Fair Oaks Station, was, along with Brigadier General William H. French's Brigade, ordered to Porter's support. Although the two II Corps brigades arrived too late to prevent a Rebel victory, they were able to mitigate what threatened to be a complete Federal disaster. As the Irishmen and the "Yankees" of the 29th crossed the Chickahominy, they saw to their front "an immense cloud of dust, through which teams and horsemen hastily broke...these teams and horsemen were followed by crowds of fugitive stragglers on foot, whose cry was that 'they had been cut to pieces.'"[15]

General Meagher deployed a company of the 69th with fixed bayonets under the direct command of Colonel Nugent. These Irishmen succeeded in "driving back the fugitives and steadying the broken masses of the Union forces." Then the II Corps brigades, with the 69th New York leading the way, marched up the hill to their front in line of battle and stiffened the broken V and VI Corps outfits which were attempting to rally at its crest. The Irishmen then marched obliquely to the right and relieved Brigadier General George Sykes' battered regular army troops. Heavily mauled in victory, the Confederates did not press their advantage. Acting as rear guard, the Irishmen withdrew south of the Chickahominy the following morning, and the men of the 88th, the last unit to cross, destroyed the bridge behind them.[16]

Following Gaines' Mill, Meagher's men returned to their fortified camp at Fair Oaks, but were soon ordered to Savage Station, as the Army of the Potomac prepared for McClellan's "change of base" retreat to the James River, which had been planned even before Gaines' Mill. As Lee's army pursued, the withdrawal turned into a nightmare of marching and fighting.

At Savage Station General Sumner ordered the 88th, led by Major

James Quinlan, to charge an enemy battery deployed across the Williamsburg Road. Quinlan led his men forward at the double quick. The Rebel gunners fired one blast at the rapidly advancing Irishmen then limbered up and took off for the rear. A superior officer noted that Quinlan "deserved the badge of gallantry to be awarded to the most brave and intrepid on the field." He was subsequently awarded the Medal of Honor. The men of the 69th repelled a Rebel probe on that regiment's picket line with rapid fire musketry then grabbed a supply of crackers and whiskey from the mountains of supplies being put to the torch. Silhouetted by firelight, the 69th slipped away in the wake of the army, rear guard of the rear guard.[17]

The worn out infantrymen of the Irish Brigade trudged into White Oak Swamp in the wake of the army's ambulance train. They marched all night, following ill-sprung creaking ambulances full of moaning wounded down sand and clay roads that glistened with a moonlit blood-glaze. Flankers thrown out to the left and right of the road sank down into the swamp and had to be pulled out of the muck by their comrades. The brigade halted on the other side of the morass and, on the morning of June 30, deployed on a hill and awaited the Rebels.

The enemy arrived that afternoon, and Rebel artillery was soon pounding the Yankee position with a fearsome barrage. Although the Irish Brigade did not suffer much from the artillery, the 69th was temporarily disorganized by a stampede of frightened mules agitated by the Confederate shellfire. With no infantry fighting to do, some of the Irish, including General Meagher, took a hand at helping the Federal gun crews. Meagher then mounted and, accompanied by his glittering staff, rode up and down the Union line.

Again the Irishmen provided the Federal rear guard as the rest of the army withdrew to Malvern Hill, an easily defensible plateau located where Union gunboats on the James could supply heavy supporting fire. As the Army of the Potomac deployed on the high ground at Malvern, the exhausted II Corps men occupied a reserve position behind the main line.

The Confederate army arrived at Malvern Hill in the morning of July 1, and General Lee, grown overconfident in the face of McClellan's timidity, ordered a series of frontal assaults on the Federal position. Successive waves of attacking Rebels were smashed by massed Union artillery and musketry. As the day waned, however, an enemy force seriously threatened the Union left flank, held by Fitz John Porter's battered V Corps. At around 5:30 PM the men of the Irish Brigade, who were busy roasting some sheep and oxen for supper, were called on to help hold the V Corps line, which appeared about to crack.

The brigade marched to the front, where General Porter personally conducted it to the danger point. As the Irish Brigade marched by, Porter was thrown from his horse but quickly remounted, gaining a cheer from the Irishmen. The general detailed the 63rd New York and the 29th Massachusetts to support some nearby artillery and ordered the 69th and 88th New York to advance into a woodlot to their front, where they encountered a line of advancing Rebels, including the 10th Louisiana. The 10th was a sort of Confederate foreign legion, with fifteen nationalities, among them Irishmen, Greeks and Italians, in its ranks.

Shortly after entering the woods, the two New York regiments, with the 69th in the first line, received a volley from fifty yards away. Porter, who had been leaving the area, turned at the sound of the firing, but seeing the 69th moving "promptly and successfully," as he later wrote, the general rapidly completed his own withdrawal unhurt.[18]

The soldiers of the 69th and 88th were less fortunate than the general, but their training and discipline held them in good stead. The Irish officers, at least, were also supplied with a "drop of the creature" supplied by General Meagher's aide, Captain Jack Gosson of the 69th. Earlier in the day the captain, a firm believer in the restorative power of liquor, commandeered the wagon of a sutler named Laffan and dragged it and its fearful owner up to the rear of the brigade line, where, under sporadic enemy artillery fire, he dispensed whiskey and brandy free of charge.

Although the 69th suffered heavily from the first Confederate volley, the regiment not only returned the fire but actually advanced while blazing away with "murderous and magnificent vollies." The well drilled 69th then filed to the right and was replaced by and fell in behind the 88th, which continued the firefight. As the Irishmen of the 69th filed out of range, a wag from the 88th sang out to them: "Ain't you glad to get out of the Wilderness." When the regiments rotated once more, the men of the 88th, now behind their sister regiment, saw a line of fire approaching the 69th's left flank in the haze of dust and gunsmoke. The Connaught Rangers advanced rapidly in oblique formation to cover the 69th's flank.

They were staggered by a volley, then poured a shower of buckshot and balls into the Rebels. A staff officer rhapsodized on the "...grand sight! These two regiments side by side like brothers in a fight, moving in and out, the one to relieve the other when their weapons became almost impossible to work." Both regiments then rushed the Rebel line and overran it in a stabbing, swinging orgy of hand to hand fighting with bayonets and musket butts. Some Irishmen dropped their muskets and went at the enemy with their bare hands! As the Confederates faltered, Colonel Eugene Waggaman, wildly swinging his 150 year old family sword over his head, bravely led his 10th Louisiana into the melee. The polyglot Louisianans, some brandishing fearsome looking Bowie knives, charged straight at the 69th, but failed to break the Irishmen. Waggaman and many of his men ended the day as prisoners of the Irish Brigade, his sword now a Celtic trophy. The ghosts of Fontenoy no doubt smiled.[19]

At dark, the men of the 69th, out of ammunition and with muskets too fouled to be reloaded without cleaning, were withdrawn, leaving the 88th to hold the line. The following day General Sumner visited the regiment, and was initially outraged by the pile of wrecked muskets within the 88th's perimeter, which he thought were damaged and thrown away by soldiers running to the rear. The general was delighted, however, when he learned they were broken because "the byes wint for the Rebs in the way they wor used to" and cracked them over the heads of the unfortunate Louisianans. Forever after the Irish regiments "were certainly favorites with the old dragoon."[20]

The Irishmen acquitted themselves well in the heavy fighting but paid a heavy price for the victory. The 69th suffered the brigade's heaviest casualties, seventeen men killed, 110 wounded and twenty-eight missing in action. The 88th was luckier, losing five men killed and twenty-eight wounded. Among the 69th's wounded was Lieutenant John Donovan of Company D, shot through the right eye by a ball which exited through his ear. Donovan was left on the field for dead; incorrectly as it turned out, for he survived both the wound and the war and was discharged in 1865. The 69th's Sergeant Bryan Haggerty, sole surviving brother of the 69th Militia's acting lieutenant colonel, was among the mortally wounded.

Also seriously wounded was Private Peter Rafferty, who had turned seventeen shortly after the battle of Fair Oaks. Rafferty refused to leave his company after being shot, was hit again, this time more severely, and

"I'll stay and fight it out." A postwar artist's rendering of the seventeen year old Private Peter F. Rafferty refusing to leave the 69th after being wounded at Malvern Hill. (*Deeds of Valor*)

carried to the rear, where he found himself "under a large tree in a bunch of fifty men, all from our regiment." Surgeon J. Pascal Smith of the 69th visited the wounded men and informed them that "his personal attendant who carried the bandages in his knapsack, had run away some days before," so he could not help them. Enraged, the wounded Irishmen showered Smith with epithets. As the surgeon slipped away into the dark, a Company B man took a shot at him.[21]

Although victorious, McClellan's legions fell back again, leaving the injured, including Lieutenant Donovan and Private Rafferty, their wounds finally washed by a steady rain, in the hands of the advancing enemy. Rafferty's multiple injuries were caused by "two bullets in the mouth and the lower part of the jaw, which smashed the bones and carried away part of my tongue. Besides this another went through my foot entering at the top and coming out at the sole." His insistence on staying in the fight at Malvern Hill, even after being wounded, won Peter Rafferty a Medal of Honor, the brigade's second.[22]

It would be a while before Rafferty picked up his medal, however. On July 4 he was transported to Richmond in a springless wagon and confined in the top floor of Libby Prison. After several weeks of neglect by the badly overburdened Confederate medical system, Rafferty and his surviving comrades finally had their wounds properly cared for by Sisters of Charity. After sixty-five days of confinement, they were exchanged.[23]

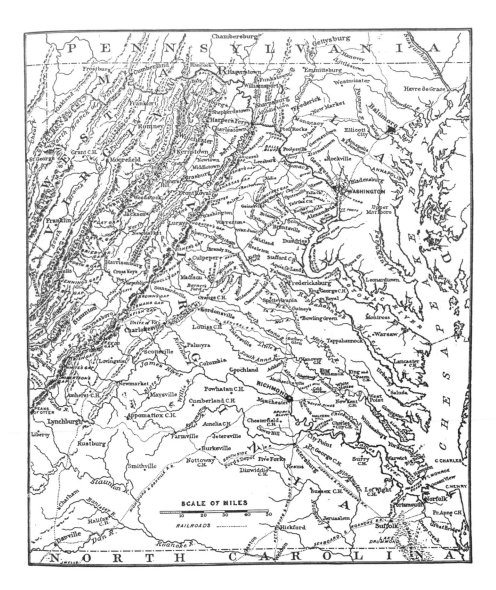

The Virginia Theater of the War

48

Chapter 3

"Sorrow Hangs as a Shroud"

In the wake of Malvern Hill the Confederates withdrew towards Richmond, but General McClellan showed little inclination to follow. Instead he continued his retreat to Harrison's Landing on the James. There his debilitated army licked its wounds and refitted, ostensibly for another campaign against the enemy capital. On July 8, President Lincoln visited the army and discussed its future with McClellan and, individually, his corps commanders. While the high command conferred, the exhausted soldiers of the Army of the Potomac rested.

During Lincoln's visit to the army, First Lieutenant James M. Birmingham, adjutant of the 88th New York, emerged from a swim in the James. With his wet underwear drying on his body, the lieutenant walked over to the 69th's camp to visit his brother. When Birmingham turned a corner and saw the president and Generals McClellan and Sumner speaking with Colonel Nugent, he ducked behind some cover and eavesdropped on the conversation. Forever after the 88th's adjutant would remember that he saw Lincoln, impressed by the Irish Brigade's sacrifices, lift a corner of the 69th's flag "and kiss it, exclaiming, 'God Bless the Irish Flag.'"[1]

While Lieutenant Birmingham's skivvies dried and the Army of the Potomac languished along the James, General Meagher and a party of his officers returned to New York to recruit for the sadly depleted Irish Brigade. The 69th, which began the campaign with 750 officers and men, suffered the most casualties from disease and battle, and only 295 soldiers answered the regimental roll call.

Meagher turned on his oratorical skills once again in a July 25 recruiting rally held at New York City's 7th Regiment Armory. One heckler cried out: "Why don't the Black Republicans go?" He was hissed into silence, however, and the response to the general was, on the surface at least, enthusiastic. General Meagher was greeted with thunderous applause as he encouraged his listeners to "come my countrymen, one more effort, magnanimous and chivalrous, for the Republic which to thousands and hundreds of thousands of you has been a shelter, a home, a tower of impregnable security...."[2]

Meagher's magic had lost some of its luster, however. The public was now fully aware of the ghastly nature of war, the civilian job market had improved and the minimal bounties offered recruits in the late summer of 1862 were not enough to tempt many men to risk their lives. In addition, Meagher's brigade had to complete for a diminishing number of Irish volunteers with his old comrade in arms, Michael Corcoran. Corcoran, freed from a Rebel prison and promoted to brigadier general, began to recruit a new brigade of Irishmen, "Corcoran's Legion," in August. There is some evidence Corcoran's supporters, and perhaps Corcoran himself, resented Meagher and others who "took advantage of my absence to break up the old Sixty-Ninth" by drawing on the old regiment to supply cadres for the Irish Brigade. Over the months of July and August, despite Meagher's pleas and $20 bounties (in addition to $100 federal bounties and city and state subsidies) subscribed by the Irish Brigade Committee, only 250 men answered the general's call.[3]

While General Meagher recruited in New York and his Irish Brigade made reconnaissance marches in the vicinity of Malvern Hill, Stonewall Jackson confronted Federal Major General John Pope in the area of the old Bull Run battlefield. Pope had organized the troops around Washington into the Army of Virginia and then advanced overland towards Richmond. With McClellan's army bottled up at Harrison's Landing, General Lee, who held the interior lines of communication, dispatched Stonewall to confront Pope, and then moved with most of his army to reinforce Jackson.

In response, elements of the Army of the Potomac were evacuated from the Peninsula to aid the Army of Virginia. Despite this assistance, most of which did not arrive in time, Pope was decisively defeated at the second battle of Bull Run. The Irish Brigade landed in Alexandria too late to be of any help to General Pope, but in time to secure the approaches to Washington as Pope's demoralized army fell back to the city.

During the course of this operation, a detachment from the 69th was detailed on picket duty in an orchard. One old soldier passed the time by using a long handled rake to demonstrate the use of the traditional Irish pike, which, he said, "was great to clear the way, and it gave the man on foot a chance against cavalry." His somewhat skeptical audience was chastened when a Confederate mounted patrol charged through the orchard and the veteran unhorsed and captured one Rebel with the rake before the others withdrew before scattered musket fire.[4]

Robert E. Lee followed up his victory over Pope with an invasion of Maryland. As Lee's Army of Northern Virginia crossed the upper Potomac, General McClellan again assumed sole command of the Federal forces in the Virginia theater and initiated a pursuit of the Rebels. Glad to be free of the humidity and mud of the Peninsula, the battle hardened Irishmen stepped off into Yankee territory in fine dry weather, swinging north through rich farm country with abundant orchards and friendly citizens. An officer expressed delight that the brigade was now "making war within the boundaries of civilization."[5]

Private Edmund Halsey of the recently recruited 15th New Jersey Infantry was impressed by the II Corps' First Division men who camped by his unit as the Army of the Potomac began its pursuit of Lee. Halsey observed that "the contrast between these troops and our men was striking." The veterans were "browned by the sun almost to blackness – no baggage but a blanket each – & not appearing to need any – a cup or tin plate their only cooking utensils – Regts. the size of one of our companies – but with muskets bright as silver. A corporal in the same New Jersey outfit characterized the II Corps survivors of the Peninsula as "...such a rough looking set you never saw in your life."[6]

Despite the fact that he came into possession of Lee's field orders revealing the scattered Rebel dispositions, General McClellan, as usual, moved his "rough looking set" after the enemy with undue deliberation. Spectators to a fight for a change, the Irishmen watched from a distance as the Federal VI and IX Corps cleared the South Mountain passes of Rebels on September 14. The Yankees drove the Confederates into the valley beyond before halting for the night. The Irish Brigade relieved the attacking force and deployed on picket duty, prepared to continue the advance in the morning. By dawn, however, the Rebels had disappeared. The Irishmen led the pursuit, following the enemy to the banks of Antietam

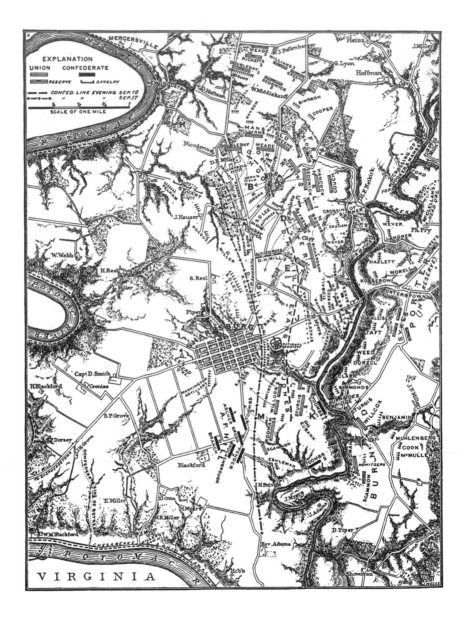

Field of Antietam.

Creek, just outside of Sharpsburg, where Lee's divided army was concentrating. As the rest of the Union army arrived, the II Corps deployed in the center of the Federal line.

General Meagher and his recruits had joined the Irish Brigade on the march and Meagher resumed command of the brigade as McClellan's army closed in on the Confederates. After some preliminary skirmishing and maneuvering followed by an artillery duel, the armies clashed at Antietam on September 17, 1862. McClellan, misusing his superior numbers, conducted a miserable battle. Starting at dawn with an advance by Major General Joseph Hooker's I Corps, the Union attack rippled down the line from the right, leaving trampled cornfields, burning farmhouses, dead soldiers and a tactical stalemate in its wake.

As he awaited the order to advance his brigade that morning, where General Meagher, who had a penchant for fine uniforms, dressed for the fight. The general was soon "gotten up most gorgeously...with a gold shoulder belt." Meagher had an orderly brush his uniform off, remarking "that 'we'd all have a brush soon.'" At 9:30 AM, with cannon and muskets banging away and smoke drifting down from the north, the Irish Brigade sloshed across Antietam Creek at Pry's Ford. Although some soldiers took their shoes off to cross the creek, others, like Corporal O'Grady of the 88th, left theirs on, afraid they wouldn't be able to squeeze swollen feet back into them. O'Grady and his comrades all filled their canteens from the cool running water, however. It would be a hot day.[7]

The II Corps, like the army itself, was committed to the battle piecemeal. General Sedgwick's Second Division, the first to go in, moved forward in line, crossing the Hagerstown Pike with its flanks open. The division moved into the West Woods, where screaming and shooting Rebels lapped around its exposed flanks and rapidly rendered it combat ineffective.

General French's Third Division initially followed Sedgwick but then veered south of the latter's ill fated route, moving towards the Confederate center. There Major General Daniel H. Hill's Rebel Division was busy frantically piling fence rails in front of a sunken road. French encountered stiff resistance, halted, then had his hands full containing desperate Rebel counterattacks. Although these sallies were repulsed, the Third Division's position was far from secure.

Then it was time for Israel Richardson's First Division to move out. As the Irish Brigade stepped out in what had become the best division in the II Corps, perhaps in the army, there was little doubt in the Irishmen's minds that they were its best brigade. They double quicked up from the ford in column past General Richardson, who cheered them on. The 69th was in the lead, followed by the Yankees of the 29th Massachusetts and then the 63rd and 88th New York. As the brigade jogged by Captain Joseph M. Knap's Battery E, Pennsylvania Light Artillery, a Keystone State gunner heard one Irishman shout "Boys, we will see some fighting now."[8]

In a cornfield in the low ground east of the Roulette farm, out of sight of the enemy and about 600 yards from the sunken road, the men of the Irish Brigade dropped their excess equipment, retaining only their muskets and cartridge boxes, and wheeled into line of battle. At the same time, Confederate reinforcements arrived for D. H. Hill. Brigadier General Ambrose R. Wright's brigade of Major General Richard H. Anderson's division filed into the Sunken Road and spilled out into the fields to the east.

When the First Division stepped out in line of battle, the Irish Brigade, led by General Meagher, was on the right. Brigadier General John C. Caldwell's brigade was on the left and Colonel John R. Brooke's brigade in reserve. The brigade's senior regiment, the 69th New York, took the place of honor on the Irish Brigade's right, making it the far right regiment of the entire division, with the 29th, 63rd and 88th to its left. As the regiments moved forward a lone horseman galloped across the brigade front. It was Father Corby, advising the men to make an Act of Contrition. No doubt many, if not most, of the New Yorkers at least, did, taking advantage of the priest's hasty absolution.

Rebel artillery located near the Piper house, a thousand yards distant, opened fire as soon as the brigade came into view. There was a fence in front of the Irishmen and as they marched they could see the enemy shells working on it, knocking splinters and fragments into the air, just as they themselves would soon be splintered and fragmented.

The left companies of the 69th, along with a number of volunteers from the 29th, ran toward the battered fence. Rebel skirmishers well in advance of the main Confederate line, which was 200 yards away, began to pepper the men working on the fence with musketry, dropping a number of them. Sergeant Samuel C. Wright of the 29th remembered that "as one would grasp a rail it would be sent flying out of his hands by rifle shots." Some Irishmen, including Corporal O'Grady and Sergeant Charles M. Grainger of the 88th, "both old British soldiers," traded their smoothbore muskets for Enfield rifle muskets and advanced to sharpshoot the skirmishers.[9]

While broken bodies and blasted wood were dragged aside from the fence line, Meagher's men laid down. On command they rose and marched up to the line, where the brigade dressed ranks as if on parade and moved forward again. As the Grayback artillery blew gaps in the advancing brigade, the New York and Massachusetts men quietly closed ranks and marched on, still not having fired a shot. More men fell, some now from small arms fire as Rebels eluding O'Grady and Grainger's men fired and fell back towards the road. Fathers Corby and Ouellet, who were riding alongside General Meagher, dismounted and administered the last rites to men who fell from shellfire and bullets. They then remounted and continued on. As his brigade closed on the enemy, Meagher stood tall in his saddle and, with shells exploding overhead, cried "Boys! Raise the colors and follow me!" And they did.[10]

Before reaching the main Confederate position, the brigade encountered Colonel Carnot Posey's Mississippi brigade, which had left the relative security of the road and pushed forward to meet the Irishmen. Posey's Rebels delivered a volley which collapsed the whole left wing of the 63rd in a heap. The regiment's right wing and the rest of the brigade blasted Posey's men with buckshot and bullets, shooting the 16th Mississippi to shreds and routing the rest of Posey's command.

Meagher wanted his brigade to hold its fire and approach the main Rebel line in the Sunken Road close enough to maximize the effect of the buckshot and ball loads in their smoothbores, fire two volleys and then charge in with the bayonet – a reprise of Fontenoy. After disposing of the Mississippians, the brigade continued its advance towards the road. Tenacious Rebels, who were under partial cover in the road while the Irishmen stood in the open, interfered with Meagher's Fontenoy scenario, however. The Irish advanced to a slight crest within thirty yards of the enemy and poured in volley after volley of buck and ball, but they could not break through the curtain of Confederate fire.[11]

After one Rebel volley, General Meagher "took off his hat and shook his sword at them." The general tried several times to initiate a

Southeastern stretch of the Sunken Road (*Battles and Leaders*)

Confederate dead of D. H. Hill's Division in the Sunken Road (*Battles and Leaders*)

bayonet charge but to no avail. Isolated individuals who charged through the gunsmoke haze to their front were never seen alive again. Color bearers fell like hay before a scythe that September morning, and the 69th lost eight of them. Captain James McGee of Company F was carrying the green banner at the end of the battle, its staff split and a bullet hole in his hat.[12]

Captain Patrick Clooney of the 88th went down with a bullet in his knee. As his men beseeched him to leave the field, Clooney, possessed by "the proud phrenzy of the fight," struggled to his feet. When the regiment's color bearer was shot down, Clooney grabbed the green banner and, using it as a crutch, limped forward encouraging his men on, until he was hit again in the chest and head by bullets and went down again – dead. Lieutenant R. A. Kelly of Kildare and the 69th, "a splendid specimen of manhood...fully six feet three inches in height" made a tall target. He and Captain John Kavanagh of the 63rd, wounded in the cabbage patch at Balingarry so long ago, had, like Clooney, expended their store of luck in this war and died in front of the Sunken Road. Sharpshooting Captain Felix Duffy of the 69th, an iconoclast who had, in turn, feuded with Corcoran, Nugent and Meagher, fell, rifle musket in hand, at the head of his company as his regiment shot it out with the 4th and 30th North Carolina.[13]

Meagher's horse went down, throwing the general hard to the earth and shaking him up so badly that he had to be carried from the field. Captain Jack Gosson's mount was also killed, but he secured another which, shot through the nose, flecked him with blood every time it breathed. The musketry roared on and the Irish held on, the only brigade of Richardson's division engaged, trading volley for volley. The only outfit with any cover at all was the 29th Massachusetts, which was partially protected by " a little hollow under the crest of a Hill while the Regts on our Right and Left [69th and 88th] were on high ground fully exposed." The fighting Irishmen were the hope of the old country, one of the best damn brigades in the new, and, on that little rise, they were rapidly being shot to tatters.[14]

But so were the Confederates. The Rebels were pinned down, with too much lead flying to run to the rear and too much lead flying for reinforcements to come up. There was no place to go, so they blazed away at the Irish, fighting – and dying – shoulder to shoulder in a country lane

Dead of the Irish Brigade, Antietam, September 19, 1862. This was the only one of Alexander Gardner's Antietam photographs that William Frassanito could not positively identify in his classic Antietam: The Photographic Legacy of America's Bloodiest Day. Although Frassanito found "no reason to doubt Gardner's original caption," he could not pin down the photo's exact location, even though he thoroughly canvassed the field directly adjacent to Bloody Land, where most of the Irish casualties occurred.

Gardner was actively recording images of the dead Rebels in Bloody Lane itself on September 19, and it is likely that these, the only dead Union soldiers he photographed in his Antietam series, were awaiting burial nearby. Most, perhaps none, of these soldiers fell in action at this exact location. The shelter halves and blankets under and over some of the bodies indicate the men were carried or dragged at least a short distance to the spot for burial in a mass grave.

The site may have been near the spot where a murderous Rebel volley cut down a large number of the men of the 63rd New York. It also may have been adjacent to the brigade's field hospital, where those who died in the hospital were no doubt buried. The man on the left appears to have had his right foot amputated -- surgically rather than traumatically. Battle detritus lays about, including a cartridge box in the right foreground and what appear to be several muskets lying on the ground in the left background. Under magnification, the belt buckle of the man farthest to the right appears to have three characters on it, which may be "SNY" (State of New York) rather than the usual "US."

If the identification is correct, and, at this point, we have no reason to believe otherwise, this image is the only one of Irish Brigade casualties. (The Huntington Library, San Marino, CA)

which was fast becoming a blood spattered road to hell. The carnage continued for over half an hour.

Israel Richardson, soon to be mortally wounded himself, was appalled at the fate of his favorite brigade. He ordered General Caldwell's brigade, which had encountered no enemy in its path, to relieve the Irish, a task performed in one of the most unique tactical operations accomplished under fire during the war. Caldwell's men moved up in column behind Meagher's brigade, and, as the Irish "broke by companies to the rear," in parade ground fashion, Caldwell's men replaced them. Caldwell's Yankees continued the firefight with the Rebels in the road and were soon joined by Colonel Brooke's brigade. The Rebels, softened up by Gaelic musketry and unreinforced, finally surrendered or took off for the rear.

The 69th New York, which had splashed across Antietam Creek that morning with 330 men, lost 196 of them, including forty-four dead and 152 wounded, twenty-seven of whom subsequently died. The 63rd had thirty-five men killed, 165 wounded and two missing, while the 88th suffered twenty-seven killed and seventy-five wounded. The brigade field hospital was established behind a haystack to the rear of the firing line. Many of the Irish wounded died and were buried there.[15]

Among the killed and wounded were seventy-five of the recruits who had just joined the brigade, men who had come, perhaps because of the charisma of the man who had led them or perhaps simply because they were out of work or looking for adventure. Whatever their motivations, their brief military careers ended in that field by the Sunken Road. The enemy, combat hardened veterans, had not paled before the "impetuosity and recklessness of Irish soldiers in a charge." Though the Irishmen had displayed at least as much tenacity and bravery as their opponents, they could reflect that the days of Fontenoy, when the enemy also fought completely in the open and were often gentlemanly enough to concede the first volley, were, at best, fast fading. Or so it seemed.

Antietam, although in actuality a bloody draw, was close enough to a victory to provide a rationale for Abraham Lincoln's Emancipation Proclamation. It also produced accolades for the survivors of the Irish Brigade. Major James Cavanaugh, who commanded the 69th while Colonel Nugent was absent on sick leave, praised Captains McGee, Saunders and Moroney and Lieutenants Duffy and Toal, all the line officers he had left. Cavanaugh also praised his enlisted men, including a private with the unusual name for an Irishman of Sucoth Mansergh. Eighty years later one student of the battle characterized the Irish Brigade fight at Antietam as "one of the most outstanding examples of extreme devotion to duty in the annals of modern military history." When the Irishmen buried their dead on the field, they stuck a rude cross over Captain Clooney's grave and carved on it, "He like a soldier fell." So did they all.[16]

Robert E. Lee's Confederates fell back into the Shenandoah Valley, and George B. McClellan's Federals tentatively pursued them. The Irish Brigade crossed the Potomac at Harper's Ferry on September 23 and camped outside the town at Bolivar Heights. As McClellan engaged in a running dispute with Lincoln over his lack of aggressiveness, the Irishmen remained camped near Harper's Ferry, in a setting which Thomas Jefferson had accurately characterized as one of the most beautiful on the North American continent.

After the rigors of the Peninsula and Antietam campaigns, they needed the rest. A brigade staff officer reported himself and the brigade as "foot sore, our clothes tattered, our shoes worn, the arms and accoutrements, so essential to action, in a very bad state." Brigade Quartermaster Haverty quickly remedied these deficiencies, however, and new clothing and equipment coupled with fine weather soon "made the days pass pleasantly and the nights without a murmur." Not so pleasantly for Jack Gosson, however. The captain, whose escapades in battle and steeplechases hinted at immortality, suffered a broken collarbone in a fall from his horse and went home on medical leave.[17]

On October 10, the 116th Pennsylvania, a recently raised but understrength regiment, joined the brigade. On the surface, the assignment of Colonel Dennis Heenan's Philadelphia outfit to the Irish Brigade seemed indicate an effort to retain the brigade's Gaelic uniqueness. Although originally characterized as the "Brian Boru United Irish Legion," Hibernian blood in the 116th diminished markedly below Heenan and Lieutenant Colonel St. Clair Mulholland, however, and the unit did not carry a green flag. A good many of the regiment's junior officers and enlisted men bore "Pennsylvania Dutch" surnames. Nonetheless, warm bodies of any ethnic derivation were welcome in the sadly depleted brigade, and the 116th would soon become one of the outfit's core regiments.

In one important matter the 116th fully measured up to General Meagher's standards. The regiment was armed with smoothbore muskets, with which the Pennsylvanians engaged in "frequent target practice down by the river bank where the boys fired away at imaginary Confederates and filled trees full of buck and ball."[18]

The 116th would soon get a crack at real Rebels. The Irish Brigade left Harper's Ferry on November 2 and, with the rest of the army, marched down the east slope of the Blue Ridge towards Warrenton, shadowed by the enemy in the Shenandoah Valley to the west. Although his men were finally marching, General McClellan was still not moving them fast enough for Abraham Lincoln, and the president relieved the Army of the Potomac's commander on November 5. McClellan's replacement, Major General Ambrose Burnside, had established a good reputation early in the war as a result of his victories in coastal North Carolina. Burnside's conduct in the more recent Antietam campaign was, however, far from praiseworthy, and he himself doubted his ability to command the army.

As in most veteran Army of the Potomac outfits, many soldiers in the Irish Brigade were extremely unhappy with McClellan's dismissal. The general's numerous failings went unrecognized by his men during his tenure of command, and McClellan, who had created that army out of the chaos following Bull Run, remained that army's favorite commander. A number of the brigade's officers attempted to resign their commissions in protest of McClellan's removal. General Meagher refused to accept the resignations, however, reminding his officers that their primary duty and loyalty was to their government and not a general, no matter how well loved.

In an attempt to steal a march on Lee and threaten Richmond, "Burn" rushed his army to Falmouth, on the Rappahannock River across from Fredericksburg. It was a hard march, and the II Corps men foraged freely across the landscape. Senior officers noted an unusual number of sheep sacrificing their lives for the Union. Brigadier General Winfield Scott Hancock, Richardson's successor as First Division commander, blamed the Irish for much of the slaughter, especially after a number of fresh sheepskins were discovered in the Irish Brigade camp. Even in the face of such strong circumstantial evidence, however, General Meagher defended his boys, claiming the men of the 5th New Hampshire had planted the fleece. Hancock was inclined to disbelief, especially after he caught some Irishmen in the act of ovinicide. On another occasion the general encountered an Irish Brigade regiment whose men were bedecked in "foraged" turnips. The exasperated Hancock screamed at the colonel, whose own turnips hung from his saddle: "Your regiment looks like a Christmas tree." Francis A. Walker, the prominent postwar economist, veteran staff officer and II Corps historian felt, however, that "there is some reason to a accept" Meagher's "indignant disclaimer," in the sheep slaughter incident. Unfortunately, Walker failed to disclose his own reasons for believing Meagher.[19]

Spurred on no doubt by generous helpings of mutton stew, the II Corps, now under the command of Major General Darius Couch, and the IX Corps, both forming General Sumner's Right grand Division, were the first Federal forces to arrive at Falmouth. The Irishmen, who had led their corps on the march, were eager to find a ford and charge the small force of Rebels on the Rappahannock's south bank. Sumner was willing to unleash them, but was restrained by Burnside's order to wait for pontoon bridges. The wait would take almost a month, and gave General Lee time to shift his army to Fredericksburg and fortify the high ground behind the town.

While the Irish Brigade waited, it lost the Protestant Yankees of the 29th Massachusetts. The Massachusetts men apparently didn't terribly mind being honorary Irishmen; the 29th's colonel felt his outfit had "added to its reputation by the mere fact of its being connected with the Irish Brigade." There were limits, however. Although General Meagher offered the 29th a green flag, the Yankees declined the honor which, they believed, would brand them as Fenians.[20]

An amicable trade was worked out with the IX Corps and, in exchange for the 29th, the Irish Brigade received the veteran 28th Massachusetts, which had fought at James Island, South Carolina and at Second Bull Run, South Mountain and Antietam. the 28th, almost as solidly Celtic an outfit as the New York regiments, had suffered through internal dissension and incompetent commanders until the arrival of Irish born Colonel Richard Byrnes, a veteran regular army soldier. Private Peter Welsh and the other men of the 28th were "glad of the change," when the 28th, originally raised for the Irish Brigade, joined the outfit. The 28th was armed with Enfield rifle muskets, a first for the brigade.[21]

As the weather grew colder, the Irish Brigade soldiers built themselves a winter camp of sturdy little tent roofed huts warmed by improvised fireplaces with barrel chimneys. Many thought they would fight no more this year. On December 2, the New York regiments turned in their tattered flags, which were scheduled to be replaced with new banners in a formal ceremony. The presentation would be especially significant, as the new flags were the grateful gift of a group of "native born" New Yorkers, some of them former members of the anti-immigrant "Know Nothing" party who had abandoned their previous prejudices in the face of the hard fighting Irishmen's loyalty to the Union. The brigade's carpenters erected a large log hall in their winter village for the festivities, scheduled for December 13, 1862.

Unfortunately, General Burnside had other plans for the Irish Brigade that day. Rumors spread among the men that a river crossing and assault on the Rebels beyond the town were imminent. After looking at the fortified heights, a prescient Irish Brigade private said to Chaplain Corby: "Father they are going to lead us in front of those guns which we have seen them placing, unhindered, for the past three weeks." Corby answered: "Do not trouble yourself; your generals know better than that."[22]

Burnside, at least, the one who mattered most, did not. On December 11, the Irishmen rose at 4:00 AM and marched to the high ground across the Rappahannock from Fredericksburg. The red legged chasseurs of the 14th Brooklyn gave a rousing cheer and a band struck up "Garyowen" when the brigade, as cocky as ever, swung down the slope towards the river. While the Irish waited, the 50th New York Engineers pushed a pontoon bridge across the Rappahannock, only to be halted midstream by Rebel Sharpshooters from Brigadier General William Barksdale's Mississippi brigade.

The Mississippians were concealed in Fredericksburg's cellars and in rifle pits dug in gardens and yards. Although successive Yankee artillery barrages battered the town and completely demoralized a Florida regiment, the deadly Mississippi rifle muskets cracked every time the engineers sallied forth upon the pontoons. Finally, Federal infantrymen from the 7th Michigan and 19th Massachusetts crossed the Rappahannock in pontoon boats, secured a bridgehead and drove the Grayback snipers out of the town.

The following day the Irish Brigade crossed over into Fredericksburg on the newly laid pontoons. Despite initial misgivings, the Irish seemed eager for the fray. General Meagher remembered that his Irish Brigade, around 1,200 strong, "never was in finer spirits and condition."[23]

The green troops of the 116th Pennsylvania stared in fascination at Barksdale's dead Mississippians strewn haphazardly like rag dolls in Fredericksburg's streets, alleys and gardens. Meagher's veterans disregarded the dead, and were more interested in scrounging boards to sleep on so they wouldn't sink in the ankle deep mud.

Although later denied, there was looting as well. A II Corps staff officer recalled "one gigantic private of the Irish Brigade wearing the white-satin bonnet of some fair 'Secesh' bride; while another sported a huge 'scoop' bonnet of the olden time. A coffee pot that would hold ten gallons, and which had evidently done duty at church festivals, was the plunder of a third member of this rollicking band; another was staggering under a monstrous feather-bed for two." Some Irishmen tore down the British consul's flag, but were ordered to return this singularly appropriate trophy to its owner.[24]

The Irish weren't the only looters, however, and some Yankees went much further. The II Corps inspector general came upon a bizzarre sight when he visited a picket reserve headquartered in "a noble house" on the outskirts of Fredericksburg. The shocked officer reported that "every man...had added to his uniform a lady's chemise taken from the well stored presses of this abode of luxury."[25]

The bizarre combination of an aurora borealis, bursting shells and burning houses created an aura almost bright enough to read by in Fredericksburg that night. Awakened before dawn on the morning of December 13, the Irishmen brushed frost off their overcoats and waited. Colonel Nugent joked with Colonel Edward E. Cross of the 5th New Hampshire that the first of them to get to Richmond would order dinner for two. Years later Nugent sadly recalled, "the dinner has never been ordered."[26]

While the brigade stood in column formation under sporadic shellfire, General Meagher and his staff distributed sprigs of green boxwood to every man, which, in the absence of the New York outfits' green flags, would identify them as members of the Irish Brigade. After what seemed an eternity, the brigade, with Meagher and his staff leading on foot, swung through the streets of Fredericksburg to the front. The

Irishmen, some waving their hats in farewell, marched almost jauntily towards the holocaust which awaited them.

The II Corps' objective that day was the high ground called Marye's Heights directly beyond Fredericksburg. The sunken Telegraph Road ran along the base of the Heights and was bordered by a stone wall. A natural defensive position, the road was occupied by two ranks of dead shot Georgians, with artillery batteries and South Carolina infantrymen ascending the slope behind them. General French's Third division had preceded the First Division into a fog and powder smoke haze and was scattered on the gray slopes beyond, twisted and broken. Then came the turn of Hancock's First Division. Colonel Samuel K. Zook's brigade of Pennsylvanians, New Yorkers and Connecticut men led off. As Zook's men approached the road, more Rebels, South and North Carolinians, swarmed into it, making a four rank deep formation that poured a deluge of musket balls on the New York general's brigade and drove it to ground.

There was only one way to follow French and Zook and that was to follow fast, at the double quick. As the Irish Brigade trotted into the maelstrom of shot and shell, an artillery round burst at the head of the 116th Pennsylvania's column, severely wounding Colonel Heenan and killing four of his men. More shells burst in and around and over the brigade column as Meagher's men advanced 200 yards forward to a canal which ringed the rear of Fredericksburg. As exploding shells filled the gray December sky over their heads, the Irish slowed down to cross the battered bridge over the canal. Once across, they formed into line of battle.

General Meagher ordered two companies of the 69th (forty-nine men) to cover his right flank in a loose skirmish formation. The rest of the brigade uncoiled with the 69th, as usual, on the right, then the 88th, 28th (carrying the only green flag that day) 63rd and 116th. All senior officers were ordered to enter battle on foot and Meagher, nursing a knee injury, did not lead the brigade any further forward. The general returned to Fredericksburg for his horse and took a position in the shell swept plain between the town and the point where his men began their attack.

The Irishmen swept forward at right shoulder shift another 150 yards from the stone wall bristling with muskets. The Rebels had blown away French's division and Zook's brigade, and they were ready for anything that came their way. They knew the Irishmen were coming, for they could see the 28th's "green flag with the golden harp of old Ireland."[27]

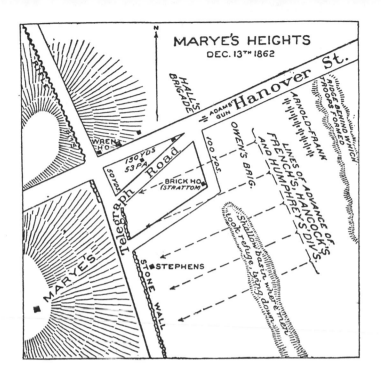

Fredericksburg: II Corps attack on Marye's Heights.

Artillery canister fire immediately blew large gaps in the Irish ranks, but, with that single green flag fluttering in the center of the brigade, the Irishmen kept on coming, over the dead and the prone survivors of previous attacks. The now ragged Irish Brigade line swarmed forward towards the Rebel ranks, until the brigade encountered a 100 yard long "fence of upright plank, spaced along timber bars and supported by equidistant posts," about fifty yards from the stone wall. As the Irish scrambled over the fence, "sheets of flame from thousands of muskets, withheld until this moment" erupted in their faces and stopped all but a few, including Major William Horgan and adjutant John R. Young of the 88th New York, who staggered forward alone and were killed within a stone's throw of the Rebels. A Confederate officer remembered that the Irish "pushed on beyond all former charges, and fought and left their dead between five and twenty paces of the sunken road."[28]

Colonel Nugent of the 69th went down badly wounded in this "living hell from which escape seemed scarcely possible." One eyed Captain John Donovan, returned from the apparent dead of the Peninsula, was hit again and knocked unconscious. The 69th's First Lieutenant Patrick Callaghan, a veteran of twenty-three years in the regular army and forty frontier fights, fell with four gunshot wounds. First Lieutenant Bernard O'Neill of the 69th was badly wounded after he picked up a soldier's musket and began to fire at the Rebels.[29]

First Sergeant John Farley of the 116th spun around, a great gout of blood spurting from his forehead and all over First Lieutenant Francis T. Quinlan. Color sergeant Tyrrel of the Pennsylvania regiment dropped to one knee when his leg was shattered by a minie ball. He was rapidly struck five more times in succession and fell, along with his banner, in a bloody heap. Lieutenant Thomas H. O'Brien of the 88th was shot through the neck, and after the fight, when he tried to eat, food came out the hole in his neck. "Strange to say, he recovered."[30]

The roar of musketry and artillery drowned out the screams of the wounded and the dying. At least some soldiers still on their feet, however, could hear James Cavanaugh, the "little major" of the 69th, screaming above the din "blaze away and stand to it, boys," until he went down badly wounded. As in the past, the Irish were in the open, but this time the enemy was behind a solid stone wall rather than a hastily erected fence rail breastwork. Lieutenant John Dwyer of the 63rd remembered someone yelling: "Lie down and fire." The order was promptly obeyed. "Fortunately...or not a man or officer would have lived."[31]

The brigade's survivors went to ground in a depression created by the removal of dirt for the erection of the board fence, which "provided the similitude of a breast-work about two feet high," and established a ragged prone firing line which spewed buckshot, balls and Enfield bullets at the stone wall. As forward elements of the 116th fell back to the cover of the ditch, the blood spattered Lieutenant Quinlan realized the regiment had left its flag along the line near the wall. He sprinted back to retrieve it, a hundred muskets blazing away at him. With the flag clasped to his chest and bullets raising geysers of mud all around him, Quinlan rolled across the ground back to his regiment.[32]

One man from the 88th crawled back towards the wall firing, and, although suffering three gunshot wounds "fired six shots with careful deliberation and fatal execution." Although surviving officers tried to extract the remains of the brigade and Meagher established a rallying point near the town, many soldiers elected to stay at the front and fight it out. Some men from the 28th Massachusetts sidled over to an abandoned brick house on the brigade's right for better cover, and delivered a hot fire from there at the Rebels. They were probably safer than those trying to retreat. The way back to Fredericksburg, swept by Rebel artillery fire, was fully as dangerous as the way forward had been.[33]

It was even more dangerous further forward. That mattered not to sergeant John Sheridan of the 88th's Company G, however. Sheridan crawled to and fro, dragging out his company's wounded before he was mortally wounded himself. Sergeant Sheridan's company lost twenty-four men killed and wounded of the thirty-two it brought to the battle.

In a last forlorn hope, General Caldwell's First Brigade swept up the slope behind the Irishmen. Although Caldwell's regiments were broken by the artillery and musketry that shattered the previous attacks, a few brave souls from his command, joined by Irishmen still on the line, charged forward to death and glory. Men continued to die along the line into the night, and fighting flared again, but the paroxysm of violence that shattered Caldwell's brigade signalled the end of the wholesale slaughter of the II Corps in front of the stone wall before Marye's Heights.

Very few Union soldiers made it past the line of the board fence in front of the stone wall; fewer still made it back. Some Rebels carried a bullet riddled Union soldier who had almost made it to the wall into their lines that night. He still hung tenously to life and, when asked his regiment, "he gasped: Sixty-ninth New York Meagher's Brigade."[34]

The town was a dangerous place as well, however. Captain John Sullivan of the 63rd left Father Corby to cross a street and, as the chaplain watched in horror, "he reached the center – ten feet from where we had been talking – a cannon ball came down the street and struck him about four inches above the knee, and cut his leg away." The captain died of his wound.[35]

At dusk the brigade's survivors fell back to the city, taking as many wounded with them as they could. When Captain Donovan, who had recovered consciousness but not the use of his left arm, ordered a retreat, "about a dozen men rose from amongst the dead" to go with him. Donovan, dodging bullets flying from front and rear, collapsed on his way down the hill, rose again, got his hat shot off and hit the dirt again. The captain crawled along until he reached some fellow Irishmen from the 69th Pennsylvania, who were caring for other Irish Brigade wounded. With their help, Donovan reached the brigade field hospital after dark.

It was the captain's last fight. He would live and serve again, but in the Veteran Reserve Corps.[36]

Captain Donovan's odyssey was typical of survivors, most of whom made their way back to Fredericksburg as best they could. Many were not as lucky as he. The dead, along with the dying, lay stiffening in the freezing dark in front of the stone wall as the temperature plummeted. Parties of rescuers who crawled out to retrieve wounded men under cover of night were raked by random musketry and suffered even more casualties.

Some of the Irish wounded received succor from Sergeant Richard Kirkland of the 2nd South Carolina, who crawled out between the lines in the afternoon of December 14 with water for those Yankees who still survived. It was not until December 15, however, that a truce permitted the evacuation of survivors still lying before the stone wall. For the second time in three months, the Irish Brigade teetered on the edge of nonexistence.

Among the brigade's dead was the color sergeant of the 69th, who wrapped the regiment's national color around his body beneath his overcoat before he died, thus saving it from capture. The Rebels did get a flag from the 69th, however. It was a camp color or guidon, left in the wreckage in front of Marye's Heights and was the only flag the regiment ever lost. Along with it, the 69th lost all of its sixteen present commissioned officers and 112 of the 173 enlisted men who assaulted the hill killed and wounded. The skirmisher detachment on the brigade's right flank suffered no losses. Only sixty-one of the men the 69th committed to the attack came out unscathed![37]

The brigade's other outfits suffered heavily as well. Captain P. J. Condon, ranking officer of the 63rd, pulled his immediate command, nine men, off the hill and encountered Colonel Byrnes, with the colors and ten survivors of the 28th on the way back to Fredericksburg. The shocked Byrnes believed his new command and the brigade it had just proudly joined were both annihilated.

Although the slaughter was not quite as bad as that, it was close to it. Stragglers continued to come in, and the five regiments mustered a mere 263 men in the immediate aftermath of the battle. The 116th, most of its officers killed or wounded, recrossed the Rappahannock under the command of Lieutenant Quinlan. The 28th lost 158 of the men it brought to the field. On parade after Fredericksburg one company of the 88th

70

mustered seven men. When a private of the same regiment standing alone was rebuked by General Sumner for not being in formation with his company, the soldier replied: "This is all my company sir." Unlike Antietam, where the disputed terrain fell to the Union, the men of the Irish Brigade felt their incredible sacrifices at Fredericksburg were for naught. One wounded officer bitterly recalled that "nothing of any good [was] obtained." Chaplain Corby summed it up succinctly, remembering that "all of us were sad, very sad."[38]

The Irishmen's heroism in a losing cause did not go unnoticed, however, even among those who might be predisposed to overlook it. A correspondent of the *London Times* wrote that "Never at Fontenoy, Albuera, or at Waterloo, was more undaunted courage displayed by the sons of Erin" than at Fredericksburg. The *Times* correspondent had, apparently, missed Malvern Hill and Antietam.[39]

Military glory often begets horror and depression in its wake, however. Following Fredericksburg one officer felt the brigade was "the most dejected set of Irishmen you ever saw or heard of." It would also, he noted, "be a sad, sad Christmas by many an Irish hearthstone in New York, Pennsylvania and Massachusetts." Another soldier felt "all is dark, and lonesome, and sorrow hangs as a shroud over us all."[40]

In the aftermath of the battle, General Meagher sent the new flags intended for his regiments home to New York, accurately claiming he did not have enough men left to protect them. The party planned for the presentation ceremony was held anyway. The brigade's officers and guests gathered in a shell shattered Fredericksburg building rocked by yet another barrage which, according to one account, scarcely disturbed the celebrants. General Hancock was a guest at the affair, and reportedly commented that "only Irishmen could enjoy themselves thus."[41]

Spirits began to rise with the season, however, and the men of the Irish Brigade decorated their winter quarters huts at Falmouth with evergreen boughs woven in the shape of harps. The Pennsylvanians of the 116th erected a Christmas tree and festooned it with tin cups, hardtack and pieces of salt pork. The Irishmen who contentedly settled into cozy winter quarters that December would never, however, for the rest of their natural lives, forget the bloody year of 1862.

The year would be remembered with sadness in New York as well. On January 16, 1863, a High Requiem Mass for the dead of the Irish

Brigade was sung by Father Ouellet in Saint Patrick's Cathedral. The mass was attended by, among others, General Meagher and his wife, the wounded Colonel Nugent of the 69th and a number of the brigade's invalid officers. It was a funeral mass for those whose coffins would never grace the center aisle of Saint Patrick's; for those "...who fell at Antietam and James River; by the Rappahannock and Chickahominy...."[42]

There were over two more years of war for the Irish Brigade – and many more requiems to come.

Chapter 4

"There They Are!"

As 1862 turned into 1863, the Irish Brigade's survivors savored the peaceful routine of their winter quarters camp at Falmouth. There was the tedium of inspections and dress parades to put up with, but after the battlefield horrors of 1862, the Irishmen were content with their lot – and glad to be alive. Boxes from home flooded the camp, and the supply chain caught up with the ragged, hungry soldiers, who received full rations and a resupply of clothing. In the 28th Massachusetts, at least, where Colonel Byrnes was concerned with the morale and comfort of his men as well as their discipline, warm "woolen gloves and legans" were issued. One enlisted man in the 28th proudly wrote that the 28th's men were "...like the Zouaves now. we have got those White Legging and have to wear them every day."[1]

Although often unlucky in its combat assignments, the Irish Brigade was fortunate during General Burnside's infamous "mud march." On January 20, 1863, the Army of the Potomac began to march upstream along the Rappahannock under an overcast sky. Burnside hoped he could outflank the Confederate positions at Fredericksburg by crossing the river at Banks' Ford above the town. That night it began to rain – and continued to rain for the next two days. The Union army became, quite literally, stuck in the mud. The II Corps, which was camped closer to the enemy than the army's other corps, was one of the last units scheduled to move out. As a consequence, the Irishmen were still in their quarters when the disastrous campaign was called off.

The abortive mud march was the last Union offensive maneuver of the winter, and the soldiers of the Irish Brigade had time to turn to more pleasant pastimes than marching or fighting. Most of these avocations reflected the Gaelic penchant for gregariousness and politics. Although many, if not most, of the Irish Brigade's original recruits (including its commander) were not practicing Fenians, the Irish Brotherhood's fire burned more brightly in the brigade's officer corps than anywhere else in the Army of the Potomac.[2]

Fenians from other regiments, like Thomas Galwey of the 8th Ohio, attended meetings of the Irish Brigade's Fenian "Potomac Circle." According to Galwey, a Fenian since 1860: "The Center of the Circle is Dr. Reynolds, Surgeon of the 63rd New York. The Secretary is Capt. John [sic] Rorty, a U. S. Artillery officer. Our meetings take place in the hospital marquee of the Irish Brigade." Doctor Laurence Reynolds, a Waterford man like General Meagher, had formerly practiced medicine in Liverpool, England. Reynolds was, by all accounts, "a hospitable man, a born raconteur, whose wit was combined with a powerful eloquence." The doctor's ability to coin a verse earned him the unofficial position of poet laureate of the Irish Brigade.[3]

After dispensing with preliminary business and reception of new members at a typical meeting, Doctor Reynolds, it was fondly remembered, stirred up a batch of milk punch: "The whiskey is good and in good quantity. Condensed milk and nutmeg are added in judicious doses by an experienced hand, who does not forget to add a little hot water just to make it mix well. Now begins the fun." The "fun" of the Circle seemed to revolve around declamations of poems and stories of "the Ould Dart," [Ireland] well lubricated with punch. Revolutionary plotting, if any, seems to have been held to a minimum.[4]

In February, with military activity at a lull, General Meagher petitioned for permission to return his brigade's three New York regiments home to recruit and refit. In support of his request, Meagher reported the combined strength of the 63rd, 69th and 88th as 340 men "for duty, including pioneers, drummers, etc.," 132 men "on extra and daily duty," and fifty-nine men "sick and wounded."[5]

Although permission to recruit the New York outfits was denied, the spring of 1863 saw a rollicking, memorable Saint Patrick's Day in the Irish Brigade. The day's celebrations were, if the diarists of the Army of the Potomac are any guide, the most significant non-combat event that army ever experienced. The Saint Patrick's Day festivities were attended

Saint Patrick's Day Celebrations in the Irish Brigade Camp, 1863.

by the luminaries of the Army of the Potomac, including Major General Joseph Hooker, who had succeeded Burnside in command following the dismal mud march. Hooker's administrative ability and attention to the basic needs of his soldiers had caused morale to soar from the depths to which it had descended under the Burnside regime. "Fighting Joe" was at the peak of his popularity.

With General Hooker's arrival at the brigade's camp, the Saint Patrick's Day ceremonies began solemnly with a "Military Mass," celebrated by Father Corby in a rustic pine bough chapel erected for the occasion. Liturgical music was supplied by army bands, and among the worshippers were contingents of soldiers in clean dress uniforms with polished leather accoutrements and burnished brass insignia and muskets, who presented arms "during the more solemn parts of the mass." The consecration was announced by cannon fire rather than bells.[6]

More secular activities quickly followed, including a "Grand Irish Brigade Steeple Chase," which gave the brigade's squireens a chance to show off their riding skills before 10,000 spectators. One officer appeared in racing colors of "scarlet, the top of his head crowned with a green velvet smoking hat, the present of his lady love." The enlisted men vied for cash prizes in mule and foot races, weight tosses, sack races and other competitions, all viewed by the visiting dignitaries from a grandstand. Impressed, General Hooker proposed "three cheers for 'General Meagher and his Irish Brigade, God Bless them.'"[7]

The brigade's officers and their brass hat guests consumed "thirty five hams, and a side of an ox roasted; an entire pig, stuffed with boiled turkeys; an unlimited number of chickens, ducks and small game. The drinking materials [for officers] comprised eight baskets of champagne, ten gallons of rum, and twenty two of whiskey." The Irish Brigade enlisted men each received a special ration of two gills of rum. No doubt many men got hold of more than their allotted share.[8]

Although the accounts of Saint Patrick's Day, 1863, fuel the legend of Gaelic fondness for whiskey, the other side of that coin, the very real Irish temperance movement, exemplified by the numerous "Father Matthew" chapters in Irish American communities, is often underreported. Chaplain James M. Dillon of the 63rd New York was a hard and fast temperance man with a good deal of influence in the brigade. Before his regiment left New York for the war, Dillon persuaded 700 soldiers to sign "the pledge" of abstinence. In order to reinforce the memories of his temperance men, Dillon had small medals cast and issued to all who swore off liquor. Needless to say, not all kept their word, as evidenced by the dangerously drunk stragglers escorted to Virginia after the 63rd's departure. Enough did, however, to provide a whiskey surplus in the regiment on those occasions when "the creature" was issued. As a result, drinkers and backsliders often turned to formal and informal fisticuffs to claim the rations of the men who adhered to the pledge. Father Corby of the 88th, not as driven a temperance advocate as Dillon, reported being "...called on at times to administer the pledge to a few who had been indulging too freely...."[9]

That March, along with the rest of the Army of the Potomac, the Irishmen received identifying corps badges. As members of the II Corps' First Division, the men of the brigade were assigned a red trefoil to wear on their hats. Interestingly, the emblem resembled a shamrock, a coincidence not lost on the Irish soldiers. As a result, at least some "men of the Irish Brigade added to the red clover leaf an emblem of the same form, though of a different color – a small, green shamrock, this denoting the brigade organization as well as the division and corps."[10]

Sporting their new badges, the soldiers of Hooker's army were on the move towards the end of April as the general initiated his plan of flanking the Confederates out of their positions at Fredericksburg. Most of the army marched upstream and crossed the Rappahannock beyond the Rebel army's left flank without opposition. The little Irish Brigade broke camp on April 27 and led the II Corps up the north bank of the river. The 88th and 63rd halted at Banks' Ford while General Meagher and the rest of the brigade advanced towards United States Ford. The 28th Massachusetts dropped off along the way to guard the road. The II Corps' First and Third Divisions followed the brigade to the fords and waited for the rest of Hooker's flanking force, which had already crossed, to move downstream and arrive opposite the crossings. On the evening of April 30, the two divisions, including the Irish Brigade, which had been marching to and fro between the two fords, crossed the river and deployed near Chancellorsville.

Although initially successful, Hooker's movement slowed as the Yankee commander encountered stiffening opposition and lost his nerve. Even though his army outnumbered the Rebels by two to one, Hooker failed to bring his numerical advantage to bear in a meaningful tactical manner.

Caught by surprise, General Lee quickly recovered. While fighting a holding action with part of his army, the Confederate commander dispatched "Stonewall" Jackson with the remainder of his men on a march to outflank the outflankers. On the evening of May 2, Jackson's men hit the exposed right of the Federal XI Corps, routing it and rolling up the Union line. Darkness, stiffening Yankee resistance and his own mortal wound eventually brought Jackson's attack to a halt. Both armies then settled down to a bloody slugging match.

The Irish Brigade, less the 88th New York, which was detached to guard the corps ammunition train along with the 5th New Hampshire and 81st Pennsylvania, was deployed at Scott's Mills, guarding the road to Banks' Ford, on May 1 and 2. the Irishmen, unaware of Jackson's flank march, were confident of Federal success. Hiram T. Nason of the 28th's Company F wrote: "I believe we will whip them at last...as a cat would a mouse."[11]

On the evening of May 2, Meagher's men heard heavy firing as Jackson's flank attack struck. The general ordered his brigade into a line of battle which halted and reorganized Yankee fugitives from the front. At 8:00 AM on May 3, the brigade, held in reserve in a Federal salient steadily shrinking under furious Rebel attacks, was ordered to the front. As the Irishmen marched past a steady stream of walking wounded, shells began to explode and bullets zip in the trees above. Sergeant Bernard McCahey of the 116th turned around, "waved his hand to the earth and air and ...exclaimed 'Good boi wurreld.'" Another soldier of the Pennsylvania regiment asked: "'What are we going in here for, Jimmy?'" Jimmy answered: "'To be after making history, Barney, for sure.'"[12]

The Irishmen would make their history that day along a line near the Chancellor House. And a terrible history it was. Major St. Clair Mulholland of the 116th had no sooner bid a cheerful good morning to Major John Lynch of the 63rd than Lynch was hit by an enemy artillery round and fell "an unrecognizable mass of quivering flesh and bones." The 69th lost ten men in the woods near Chancellorsville, as the Chancellor House burned in the background. The 88th, which was rushed to the front and fought under the command of Colonel Cross of the 5th New Hampshire, also suffered severely.[13]

Enemy artillery fire was so heavy that the guns of the 5th Maine Battery, deployed in an orchard by an open field on the brigade's left, were silenced by a murderous counterbattery fire that killed Captain George Leppine, the battery commander, and a number of his men and wounded many others. The air around and above the battery was full of explosions and bits and pieces of horses, men, guns, exploding caissons and apple blossoms. Most of the surviving Maine men abandoned their guns.

As the Yankee perimeter shrunk under Rebel pressure, the Irish Brigade was ordered to fall back. During the course of the withdrawal, a party of men from the 116th wheeled off the 5th Maine's abandoned artillery pieces by hand, saving them from the advancing Rebels. The Pennsylvanians left their muskets on the line in order to have their hands free to move the cannons. When a party returned to retrieve the muskets, they found the position on the verge of being overrun by the enemy and discretely withdrew. Mulholland's men rearmed themselves with guns dropped by other troops as they retreated. The 88th, following the bri-

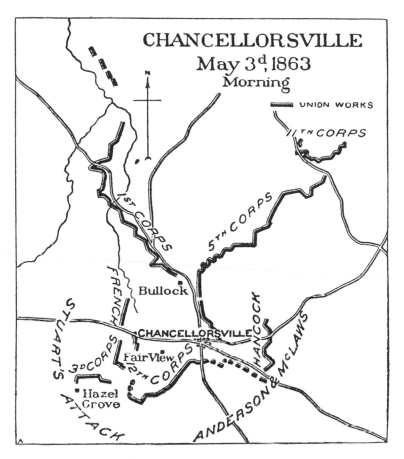

Chancellorsville, May 3, 1863

gade tradition of being rear guard of the rear guard, was one of the last Union regiments to leave the Chancellorsville battlefield.

General Hooker recrossed the river on May 4. The Irish Brigade, which began the campaign filled with hope in bright spring sunlight less than a week before, retreated to the crossing in a driving rain. The Irishmen slipped down the muddy south bank of the Rappahannock, trudged across a pontoon bridge and then scrambled up the slick slope on the other side. Soon they were back where they started.

Among the Union's Chancellorsville dead was Lieutenant William O'Donohue, formerly of the 69th Militia. Captured at Bull Run, O'Donohue escaped north with James McKay Rorty and, like him, received

"General Meagher's brigade under fire – dragging the guns of the Fifth Maine Battery off the Battlefield." An artist's conception of the 116th Pennsylvania's heroics at Chancellorsville. (Bud Scully Collection)

a commission in the artillery. O'Donohue was killed while commanding three guns of the 4th U. S. Artillery covering the Federal withdrawal.

Following the fight the Irishmen lost their corps commander. Darius Couch, a competent officer depressed by the defeat and needless slaughter of his men, resigned, to be replaced by the First Division's commander, General Hancock. Upon Hancock's elevation, Brigadier General John Caldwell took command of the First Division. More important to the Irish, however, was the resignation of General Meagher, who was frustrated by the government's denial of permission to take his decimated regiments home to recruit. On May 19, almost a year since they first marched into combat at Fair Oaks, the survivors of the brigade formed in hollow square to bid their commander goodby. The men cheered, then shook Meagher's hand, whereupon the general who created the Irish Brigade rode out of its combat history forever. His departure was not, however, the end of the brigade's story.

Some thought it might be. The once mighty Irish Brigade was a sadly diminished organization. The 116th Pennsylvania, understrength from the start, was consolidated into a four company battalion in January, 1863. In order to retain command of the unit, Lieutenant Colonel Mulholland had to accept a reduction in rank to major. Following Meagher's departure, the New York regiments were consolidated into three two company battalions. Each battalion was allotted one field and six company grade officers, and all other shoulder straps were discharged.

Many other outfits in the same condition were consolidated with other units and lost their identities. The Irish Brigade and its regiments, small as they were, remained in existence, however, and spent the next month on picket duty along the Rappahannock. The brigade's combat strength was diminished a bit more when Company A of the 116th was assigned to duty as division headquarters guard.

On June 14, 1863, Colonel Patrick Kelly of the 88th New York, "a brave, gentle, splendid soldier" and, like many of the brigade's officers, an alumnus of the 69th New York Militia, led the men of the Irish Brigade north from the Rappahannock line. They were heading north to find the Rebels. In the wake of his Chancellorsville victory, General Lee invaded the north, and the Army of the Potomac began a belated series of forced marches in pursuit. The Irish Brigade's tramps across Virginia and Maryland that June were some of the hardest the men endured in their

Lieutenant Colonel St. Clair Mulholland, 116th Pennsylvania. Mulholland was demoted to major when the 116th was consolidated into four companies in January, 1863, then promoted to colonel when the regiment was reorganized in the spring of 1864. This picture of him as a lieutenant colonel was probably taken when the regiment was raised in the fall of 1862.

entire period of service. At the end of one day, a battalion commander turned around and saw he was leading but one man; all the rest had fallen out along the road, exhausted.[14]

After June 28, the Irishmen marched under a new army commander. Hooker, who had fallen out of favor following his Chancellorsville defeat, was maneuvered into resigning the command of the Army of the Potomac and replaced by Major General George Gordon Meade. Although a conservative commander, Meade was forced to give battle on July 1, when Yankee cavalry and then his I and XI Corps collided with the Rebels at Gettysburg.

On June 30 the Irish Brigade rested and mustered for pay, giving sorefooted stragglers a chance to catch up. The following day, as Brigadier General John Buford's horse soldiers deployed west of Gettysburg, the Irish Brigade began its march to Taneytown, arriving there in late afternoon. When word arrived that Major General John Reynolds, the I Corps commander, had been killed and that the men of his corps and the XI Corps were fighting for their lives against a growing number of Rebels, General Hancock sped north to assume command of the engaged Federal forces. The II Corps continued its march on into the night, halting about three miles south of Gettysburg, where the First Division deployed across the Taneytown Road, with its left flank near Big Round Top.

The men of the Irish Brigade were awakened at 3:30 AM on July 2, and, after a hasty breakfast, marched north for about a mile and halted again on the Taneytown Road until dawn. Around 7:00 AM the II Corps moved again, this time to the west of the road and up Cemetery Ridge, where the corps deployed on the left of the battered I and IX Corps. Following the line of the gradually descending ridge, the II Corps' left flank linked with the right of the III Corps, which prolonged the Federal position almost a mile to the south towards Little Round Top. The ground on the First Division's front sloped gently away towards Plum Run and, beyond, the Emmitsburg Road. Some Irishmen laid down to get some sleep as the sun rose in the sky, while others talked, played cards or wrote letters. As the morning, and then the afternoon, slipped away, the heat increased and a number of soldiers wandered down to Plum Run to refill their empty canteens.

Late that afternoon Major General Daniel Sickles decided to improve his III Corps' position by moving the corps' two divisions forward

Colonel Patrick Kelly, 88th New York. The Galway born Kelly joined the 88th as lieutenant colonel in 1861 and was subsequently promoted to colonel. He commanded the Irish Brigade following Chancellorsville until early 1864 and resumed command when Colonel Byrnes was mortally wounded at Cold Harbor. He was killed in action leading the brigade at Petersburg on June 16, 1864. (NYSAG/USAMHI)

This statue on the Gettysburg Battlefield commemorates Father Corby's famous absolution of July 2, 1863. An identical statue stands on the campus of the University of Notre Dame. Irreverant Notre Dame students have given the chaplain the nickname "Fair Catch Corby," since his upraised right hand resembles the signal for a football "fair catch." Father Corby served two terms as president of Notre Dame: 1866-1872 and 1877-1881. (Dr. David Martin)

towards the Emmitsburg Road. Sickles' corps eventually occupied a salient which ran south along the road, then doglegged across a peach orchard to a rocky ridge that bordered a wheatfield and culminated in the helter skelter glacial stoneyard of Devil's Den. The First Division soldiers watched Sickles' men go, and General Hancock, visiting his old outfit, predicted the advancing Yankees would soon come tumbling back.

Unfortunately for the Federal army, Hancock was right. Sickles' salient made the Confederate offensive plan to attack the Union left easier. Hit in front and flank with a heavy artillery barrage followed by advancing infantry as evening approached, the III Corps was severely shaken. General Hancock, who was ordered to bolster the endangered corps, di-

Absolution under fire. Artist Paul Wood's somewhat romanticized rendering of Father Corby's famous Gettysburg general absolution. (Snite Museum of Art, University of Notre Dame)

rected General Caldwell to prepare his First Division to come forward. When Colonel Kelly called his troops to attention, the Irishmen heard a steadily increasing drumfire of musketry rolling across their front. After a false start to the front, the brigade returned to its position. The tension increased.

As the brigade prepared once more to go into battle, Father Corby stepped up onto a rock and the men fell to their knees. Corby, his statue still frozen in time, has gained eternal fame for absolving his Irishmen at Gettysburg. The chaplain could see thousands of soldiers, however, and his general absolution was "intended for all – *in quantum possum* – not only for our brigade, but for all, North and South, who were susceptible of it and who were about to appear before their Judge." Major General Hancock – the Superb – Hancock the profane – sat his horse and doffed his hat in reverence. The scene, which no doubt evoked racial memories of open air masses and hedge schools in the days of the Penal Code, remained frozen in the memories of its participants down all the days of their lives.[15]

With the arc of Father Corby's hand scribing a cross in the air still fresh in their minds, the Irish regiments fell into column and moved out, following Colonel Cross' First Brigade of New Hampshire, New York and Pennsylvania men down the gentle slope of Cemetery Ridge due south, past the Weikert farm, towards Little Round Top. The division's remaining two brigades fell in behind Colonel Kelly's veterans. As Caldwell's division moved south, Colonel Zook's Third Brigade, the last in line, was detached by a III Corps staff officer and rushed into the Trostle Woods, off to the division's right.

Caldwell, who seems to have been unaware that his tail end brigade was gone, was ordered by V Corps commander Major General George Sykes to swing his Division to the west, in an effort to restore the dissolved III Corps line in the Rose Wheatfield. Caldwell pushed his brigades towards the enemy as fast as he could turn them.

The Irishmen splashed across Plum Run and then pushed northeast through Trostle's Woods and southwest into Rose's field of ripening wheat. Here Kelly shook his brigade out of column and into a line of battle and angled west, pulling away from Cross' Yankees. Kelly's men advanced towards Stony Hill, which overlooked the Wheatfield and dominated the ground stretching northeast from Devil's Den. Zook's Brigade, which had passed through two battered V Corps brigades, reappeared out

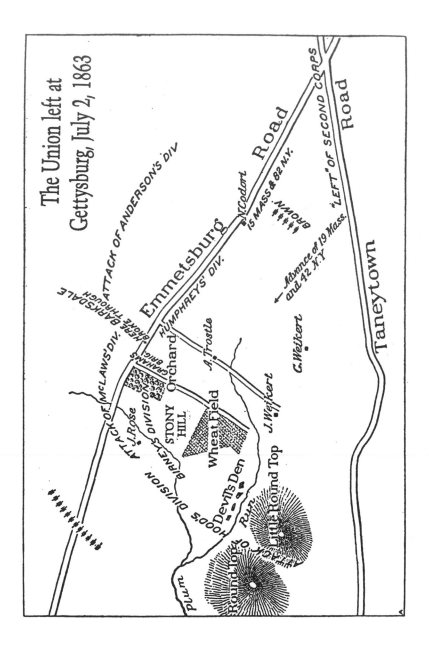

The Union left at Gettysburg, July 2, 1863

of the Trostle Woods marching somewhat forward and off to the right of the Irish. Colonel John Brooke's Fourth Brigade, Caldwell's reserve, straddled the rear of Cross and the Irishmen. The Irish Brigade line advanced with the 116th on the brigade right, then the 28th, 63rd, 69th and 88th to the left of the Pennsylvanians. As the Irish moved forward, beaten III Corps men passed through their line on the way to the rear. Kelly, whose tiny brigade scarcely occupied a 150 yard front, had no reserves and no idea how many Rebels were ahead of him. It was around 5:30 PM.

Elements of Brigadier General Joseph B. Kershaw's South Carolina brigade occupied the Irish Brigade's objective. The Carolinians of the 3rd and 7th Regiments, with at least part of their vision obscured by vegetation and powder smoke, were concentrating on the advance of Zook's line, which partially masked Kelly's advance. As a result, the Confederates on the crest of Stony Hill were apparently unaware of the Irishmen's approach. Conversely, the Irish didn't know where the Rebels were. They would soon find out.

The men of the Irish Brigade entered the woods at the end of the Wheatfield and started up the hill, struggling to maintain their battle line amidst the jumbled landscape of trees and rocks. Finally apprehending the threat, the Rebels fired a hasty ill aimed volley that zipped over the Irishmen's heads. A soldier in the 116th caught a flash of butternut in the trees ahead and cried: "There they are." The brigade, thirty yards downhill from the enemy, returned the compliment with buckshot and musket balls.

The Irish Brigade's New York and Pennsylvania regiments were still armed with smoothbore muskets loaded with "buck and ball," which Major Mulholland of the 116th characterized as "a wretched ammunition for distant firing,...[but] just right for close hand to hand work." And close work it was. "Little Jeff" Carl of the 116th shot a Rebel six feet from his musket's muzzle, and officers drew their revolvers and joined actively in the fight.[16]   It was pay back time for Antietam and Fredericksburg, and the unlucky recipients were the men of the 7th South Carolina Infantry, which had entered the battle with almost as many men on its rolls as the whole Irish Brigade. After a series of volleys, the brigade rolled over the Rebels, capturing a number of prisoners and driving the rest of the Carolinians off the hill and into the Rose farm fields. At least one of the Irish units, the 28th Massachusetts, descended the slope towards the farm but was caught in a vicious crossfire and fell back up the hill. Zook's brigade was thrown into some disarray as well. Zook himself went down mortally wounded as the attack began. His right flank regiment, the 140th Pennsylvania, had its right flank up in the air, exposed to any Rebels who might get around it.

As the Irishmen approached Stony Hill, Cross' brigade became involved in a firefight with General George T. Anderson's brigade of Georgians several hundred yards to the Irishmen's left rear. Cross' brigade suffered severely, as most of his men fought in the open field while the Georgians had a stone wall for cover. If Cross' men fell back, the Irish Brigade would be as exposed as the 140th's right. The Irish position was, at best, tenuous.

General Kershaw hoped to make it more so. After rallying his men near the Rose house and barn, Kershaw rode for help from Brigadier General Paul Semmes' brigade of Georgians. Semmes soon had other problems, however. As Kelly and Zook fought their way up Stony Hill, Caldwell ordered Brooke's brigade forward through the wheat to relieve Cross' beleaguered outfit. Brooke's Connecticut, Delaware, New York and Pennsylvania men, last reserve of the First Division, swept southwest across the Wheatfield with fixed bayonets, passed through Cross' position and drove Anderson's men from the stone wall into and through the Rose Woods. Brooke finally halted 150 yards forward of the Irish left, where his men engaged in a pointblank firefight with Semmes' Georgians, halting, then pushing them back.

Although the red shamrocks of the First Division had swept all before them, trouble was in the offing. Both of Caldwell's flanks were now up in the air, and he no longer had a reserve. Then the III Corps position along the Emmitsburg Road and in the Peach Orchard collapsed. As General Barksdale's Mississippians cleaned out the Peach Orchard, General William Wofford's brigade of 1,400 Georgians swept down the Wheatfield Road, picking up Kershaw's men and driving towards the 140th Pennsylvania's open flank. On the other end of the division line, Rebels began to lap around Brooke's position, which was dangerously in advance of the rest of the division. General Caldwell desperately rode right then left in an attempt to find other units to protect his flanks. What he got was too little, too late.

Caldwell felt the radically changing situation forced him "to fall back or have my command taken prisoners." With Confederates coming down on both flanks, the general's men anticipated his command and began to retreat on their own, as it became evident that the jaws of a trap were about to close around them.[17]

Of necessity leaving their dead and badly wounded behind, Colonel Kelly's Irishmen rapidly retreated down Stony Hill and into the Wheatfield, firing all the while. There they became mixed up with elements of Zook's and Brooke's brigades and suffered severely from Rebel crossfire. Although Caldwell's retreat saved his outfit from destruction, the First Division left a bloody trail of dead and wounded across the Wheatfield and all the way back to Cemetery Ridge. Among the latter was Martin "Jersey" Gallagher of the 116th, who fell in the Wheatfield with a broken leg, only to be hit by four more bullets. Many of the injured were taken prisoner or died over the following forty-eight hours.[18]

There would be more blood shed in that field before the end of the day, and the Rebel assault tide lapped the base of Cemetery Ridge before it was halted by increasing Union resistance and the dark. The exhausted Irishmen were assigned a reserve position on the ridge, about 200 yards south of the famous copse of trees which would serve as the focal point of General Longstreet's massive assault of July 3, popularly known as "Pickett's Charge." Although Kelly's men did no close range fighting that day, the survivors of the 28th Massachusetts fired some long range Enfield vollies at the advancing Rebels to their right front. A number of Confederates came into the Irish Brigade lines with hands raised rather than risk life and limb retreating across the bullet and shell swept field to their rear.

Gettysburg cost the Irish Brigade dearly. Although the number of casualties suffered by the five little regiments seems small by comparison with the losses of other units on the field, or their own losses in previous battles, the brigade's percentage of men killed, wounded and missing was quite high. Most were lost in the retreat across the Wheatfield. The 69th New York went into the fight at Gettysburg with six officers and sixty-nine enlisted men, out of the 107 men carried on the regimental rolls. Twenty-five men, more than a third of those engaged, became casualties. Almost fifty percent of the men in the 28th Massachusetts, the brigade's largest regiment, were killed, wounded or missing in action.

The soul of the 69th New York Militia suffered one additional loss at Gettysburg. On July 2, James McKay Rorty, now a staff captain, was detailed to temporary command of Battery B, 1st New York Artillery, which contained a section of guns manned by soldiers from the old 2nd New York Artillery Battalion. That afternoon, as Battery B fired in support, Captain Rorty had the opportunity to watch his old comrades in action against the Carolinians on Stony Hill. Battery B ended the day's fighting on the gun line which finally helped halt the Rebel attack. The following morning the battery moved to the center of the Union position on Cemetery Ridge.

During the artillery duel which preceded Pickett's Charge, three of Battery B's guns were dismounted and the battery suffered a number of casualties. To keep his remaining cannons firing, Rorty himself joined a gun crew. When the Confederate assault ebbed away, the second ranking Fenian in the Army of the Potomac was found dead amidst the wreckage of his battery.

On July 13, 1863, draft riots erupted in New York. The rioters, incensed at what they perceived as an inequitable conscription law which essentially exempted the wealthy, who could buy a $300 exemption or pay substitutes to go in their places, were predominantly Irish laborers. Colonel Nugent of the 69th, who resigned his field commission after being wounded at Fredericksburg, had reverted to his regular army rank of captain and was acting as provost marshal in charge of New York City's draft. Irish war hero though he was – and perhaps because he was – the mob attacked Nugent's house in the Yorkville section and burned it to the ground. The colonel's broken sword turned up a week later on the Upper East Side, a child's plaything, jewels pried from its hilt.

The 69th New York State Militia, which mustered a number of Bull Run veterans and convalescents from the Irish Brigade it its ranks, was performing a stint of active duty in Baltimore under the "little major," James Cavanaugh, when the riots broke out. The officers of the regiment quickly drafted a series of resolutions expressing "regret and indignation" as the actions of the mob. They attributed the excesses of the rioters to "banded thieves from other cities" and volunteered to return home to repress the insurrection. By the time the regiment came back to New York, however, the riots had smoldered out.[19]

It has been erroneously asserted that elements of the Irish Brigade returned to New York at the time of the riots, but the brigade remained on duty with the Army of the Potomac. A number of Irishmen in the ranks, who had risked all for the Union, were enraged by the disturbances, however. New Yorker Peter Welsh of the 28th Massachusetts fumed at the "disgraceful" riots. Welsh, now a color sergeant in the 28th, believed the authorities should "use canister freely" against the rioters and that the leaders of the insurrection should "be hung like dogs." Along with other Irish soldiers, Welsh was angered and embarrassed at the ethnic composition of the rioters and, exasperated, exclaimed "god help the Irish."[20]

Sergeant Welsh and his comrades left Gettysburg behind them when General Meade's army, as battered in victory as Lee's in defeat, cautiously pursued the retreating Rebels. On July 9 the Irish Brigade marched through Frederick, Maryland, to the cheers of citizens. The Irishmen crossed the old Antietam battlefield on July 10 and that evening encountered the enemy at Jones' Crossroads. Meade cautiously probed the Rebel defenses for several days, until General Lee withdrew his army across the Potomac. The Federals followed Lee into Virginia, where both exhausted armies warily watched and sparred with each other. Daily foraging was good in northern Virginia that high summer of 1863. The soldiers of the Army of the Potomac, and the Irish were no exception, noted the abundance of fruits in their diaries. The Irishmen, needless to say, were delighted with an abundance of cabbage. The health of the army improved notably.

The Irish Brigade got in as much hard marching as good eating as summer faded into autumn and Generals Meade and Lee maneuvered across northern Virginia. With both armies weakened by the detachment of troops to the western theater of war, each commander warily sought a decisive advantage. On one occasion, as Meade and Lee raced towards Washington, the Irish Brigade, taking up its old role as rear guard, covered seventy-six miles in fifty-six hours. On November 9, during a pause between hard marches, General Meagher visited the brigade and "on several days there was a first class jollification."[21]

In late November, Meade crossed the Rapidan in an attempt to outflank Lee, initiating the final campaign of the year. Poor Federal coordination and excellent Confederate defenses led to a stalemate in the area of Mine Run. On November 27, 1863, as the Irish Brigade awaited an attack order against substantial Rebel field fortifications that fortunately never came, some of the brigade's officers dropped old animosities to fraternize with "Colonel Peel, of the British Grenadiers, son of Robert Peel, a guest of General Meade." The British officer traded some of his "excellent cigars" for "good whiskey" from Irish canteens, and "the interview was enjoyed by all." Declining to attack a virtually impregnable enemy position, Meade ordered his army back over the river, where, on December 5, 1863, the Irish Brigade went into winter quarters at Stevensburg, three miles from Brandy Station.[22]

Chapter 5

"We Run This Machine Now!"

Over the winter of 1863-1864 the Federal government launched a recruiting campaign to retain veterans in the service. Most of the men who joined the army in 1861 were due to be discharged during 1864, and the loss of these experienced soldiers would be catastrophic to the Union cause. Surprisingly, despite all that they had been through, a large number of Irish veterans from the 28th, 63rd, 69th and 88th reenlisted. The extremely large bounties and generous furloughs offered as an inducement were no doubt a determining factor in the decisions of many old soldiers, as was a desire to see the thing through to the end. Reenlistees from the three New York regiments returned home in early January to enjoy well earned furloughs and recruit their ranks. Those who declined the government's offer remained on duty in Virginia.

Since the original recruits of the 116th Pennsylvania had volunteered in 1862, they were not offered the opportunity to reenlist. The state of Pennsylvania did, however, make a significant effort to restore Major Mulholland's battalion to regimental strength by recruiting six new companies, some from as far away as Pittsburgh. Mulholland was commissioned colonel of the reborn 116th.

Recruiting for the 28th Massachusetts proved slow until Colonel Byrnes of the 28th and four of his officers returned to Boston on a regimental recruiting mission in mid-February, 1864. Between January and May the 28th enlisted 326 new men, most of them after Byrnes took over recruiting. A number of the 28th's veterans reenlisted as well, and the regiment was in fine shape for the spring campaign.

As the New York regiments drew increasing numbers of recruits, some officers discharged in the previous year's consolidation rejoined their outfits. Deserving enlisted men were also commissioned from the ranks. On January 16, 1864, the Irish Brigade's New York officers, old and new, gave a banquet for their enlisted men. The reenlisted veterans of the 63rd, 69th and 88th met at New York city hall and, led by a band, marched uptown to Irving Hall, where General Meagher made a rousing recruiting speech. Meagher, at his oratorical best, told the battle hardened gathering that "history has no power to bestow upon me any higher distinction than that I have been the general in command of the Irish Brigade." Other officers and non-commissioned officers proposed a series of toasts including salutes to dead comrades whose "memory shall remain for life as green in our souls as the emerald flag..." and, "The Irish Brigade; what there is left of it."[1]

Provost Marshal Nugent did all he could to stimulate recruiting interest in his former command, and with some success, despite the pronouncement of the Boston Pilot a year prior that "the Irish spirit for the war is dead! Absolutely dead!" Irish opposition to the conflict was growing, however. After an initial burst of enthusiasm, the Fenian movement had split over the war, and, when prominent pro-war Fenian General Michael Corcoran was killed in a riding accident on December 22, 1863, the anti-war forces in the movement assumed the ascendancy.[2]

An increasing flow of Irish immigrants was no doubt helpful to the brigade's recruiters, however. Although there is no definitive proof for Confederate allegations of a major Federal recruiting drive in Ireland, large numbers of Irishmen besieged American consuls for passage to the United States. Available evidence suggests that at least one consul proposed distributing free tickets to some of these men. Many young Irishmen hoped to escape the grinding poverty and prolonged depression of rural Ireland and find employment in the the booming job market produced by Union mobilization. Others, despite the wholesale opposition to the Union cause expressed by Irish newspapers and opinion makers, probably emigrated with enlistment in mind.

There was no lack of warning of the wiles of recruiters, much of it exaggerated, to emigrants. Priests of diminishing parishes preached against emigration from their pulpits. A pamphlet attributed to the British government provided graphic examples of American anti-Catholicism, including an alleged incident of a priest deliberately marooned in a swamp to be devoured by alligators and snakes. The pamphleteer advised male emigrants that within forty-eight hours of landing they would "find themselves 'soldiering' in the swamps of the Carolinas or on the sand bars of Charleston," presumably within reach of reptiles even Saint Patrick was powerless against.[3]

In 1863, Irish Republican Brotherhood founding member Jeremiah O'Donovan Rossa termed stories attributing massive Irish immigration to American recruiters as a "landlord English lie" and castigated the editors of the *Cork Examiner* who "perhaps unwittingly, circulate the lie." Rossa contended that grinding poverty created by oppressive landlords was the root cause of emigration. There was, no doubt, a good deal of truth in this, especially since the country had experienced several bad harvest years in a row. Announcements of collections and benefits to assist poverty stricken rural Ireland were a staple news item in the Irish American press. Soldiers serving in the Irish Brigade often contributed to these causes through their chaplains.[4]

There was at least one incident of genuine recruiting chicanery, however. Patrick H. Finney recruited over a hundred young men in Dublin and Galway, ostensibly to work on American railroads and construction projects. Passing through Nova Scotia, Finney and his charges landed in Portland, Maine in March of 1864, where some of the "able bodied young Irishmen" were "cajoled or starved or drugged with villainous liquor into enlisting," in the 20th Maine Infantry. The remainder were brought to Charlestown, Massachusetts, where they were warehoused on the premises of Finney's partner, Jerome G. Kidder. After supplying his potential recruits with "liquor in quantities," Kidder advised the Irishmen that the Irish Brigade's 28th Massachusetts was the best regiment for them. At this point the scheme was uncovered, became front page news in the Irish American press and unraveled. Although some joined the army anyway, most of Finney's crew found civilian employment with help from Boston's Irish community. One Dubliner, John Connor, warned the home folks to advise young men that if they should "come on the same expectation that we came on, it would be the greatest suck in they ever got and it would be the same for us only for the Irish People here [Boston]."[5]

Despite being characterized as a United States government recruiter by British authorities in Ireland, Finney and his partner Kidder were actually "substitute brokers," or entrepreneurs hoping to make a tidy profit providing substitutes for Americans who were drafted or volunteers to fill enlistment quotas.

Many immigrants who donned the blue voluntarily probably did not leave the old country with the intention of becoming soldiers. One Union recruit, Thomas McManus, wrote home that he was not "forced to list up," but, "by 'Gor' the bounty was very tempting and I enlisted the first day I came here." His $700 enlistment bounty was ten years' wages in Ireland! No doubt with at least some men like McManus in the ranks, the New York Irish Brigade regiments returned to the Army of the Potomac in February. The 69th Battalion, which left Virginia with just A and B Companies, returned to the Army of the Potomac with six companies, A, B, C, F, G and K. The 63rd battalion enlisted a number of new men in its A and B companies and also raised new C, D and E Companies in New York City and Brooklyn. Company F joined the 63rd in the field in June. The 88th Battalion brought new companies C, D, and E back to Virginia with its Companies A and B.[6]

Recent immigrants, American born raw recruits and veterans of the old line brigade regiments were not the only soldiers to fill the Irish Brigade ranks that spring of 1864. New York had enlisted a number of two year service regiments in 1861, and all the Union states had raised nine months service "militia" outfits in 1862. These soldiers provided a pool of already trained men, and many, attracted by local, state and Federal bounties that at times approached $1,000, reentered the service in 1864. One of these men, William H. Reid, who had previously served in the 11th New York, found himself in Boston in 1864 and joined the 28th Massachusetts.

Saint Patrick's Day was celebrated in the Irish Brigade camp in March of 1864 "with considerable spirit and something of the usual eclat." A pretty fair steeplechase" entertained a bevy of visiting officers and some ladies and was followed by the usual mule, sack and foot races and other events for enlisted men, a band concert and a banquet catered by the sutler of the 28th Massachusetts.[7]

Aside from the Saint Patrick's Day festivities, there was little time for relaxation that spring, as the brigade worked to integrate the new recruits, about 80% of its strength, into the ranks. Veterans drilled the new men daily and a division drill was held on April 26. Although impressive, the exercise, which culminated in a cheering Irish Brigade bayonet

Brigadier General Thomas A. Smyth. Smyth, born in Fermoy, County Cork, was a Wilmington, Delaware carriage maker when the war broke out. He rose through the ranks to become colonel of the 1st Delaware Infantry and was assigned to temporary command of the Irish Brigade, which he led from February through May, 1864, when he turned over command to the returning Colonel Richard Byrnes of the 28th Massachusetts. Promoted to brigadier general in September, 1864, Smyth was mortally wounded on April 7, 1865. He was the third man who had commanded the Irish brigade to die from battle wounds and the last Union general to die in the Civil War.(MASS/MOLLUS/USAMHI)

charge, bore little relationship to the tactical problems the Irishmen would encounter in the weeks ahead.

They would face those problems under the watchful eye of newly minted Lieutenant General Ulysses S. Grant. Grant, elevated to command of all the Union's armies, made his headquarters with General Meade's Army of the Potomac during the war's final year. The Potomac army's

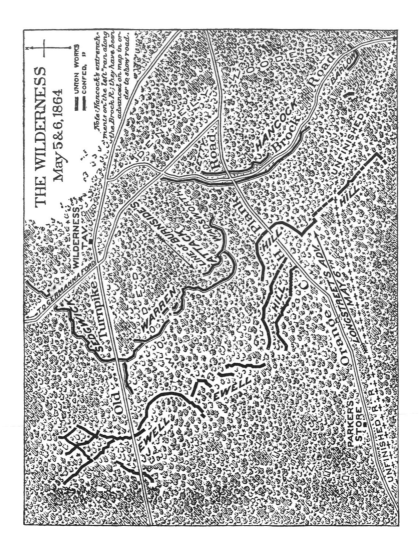

THE WILDERNESS
May 5 & 6, 1864

UNION WORKS
CONFED, D

Note: Hancock's entrenchments on the left "ran along the Brock R.; they have been advanced on map in order to show road.

100

role in Grant's overall plan was to strike General Lee's Army of Northern Virginia and stick with it until the Rebel army was destroyed. It was a mission easier assigned than fulfilled. The men of the Irish Brigade were assigned a new leader, County Cork born Colonel Thomas Smyth, the former commander of the 1st Delaware Infantry, to lead them on that mission.

Rebuilt and eager for action, Colonel Smyth's Irish Brigade, the Second Brigade of Brigadier General Francis C. Barlow's First Division of the II Army Corps, was ready to take on Grant's daunting assignment. The brigade broke camp at Stevensburg on the evening of May 3, 1864, and crossed the Rapidan River at Ely's Ford the following morning. After a three hour halt, the Irish resumed the march, arriving at the old Chancellorsville battlefield that afternoon.

The brigade camped near the ruins of the Chancellor House and the scene of the previous May's fight. The apple trees were in bloom once more, and the Irishmen retraced their steps, walking over the ground where the 116th rescued the guns of the 5th Maine Battery. Later, some would remember their comrades' final resting places covered with a blanket of wildflowers and dropped blossoms; others viewing the same scene recalled thinly covered graves with protruding bones and the disinterred remains of men, horses and broken equipment scattered haphazardly across the forest floor.

On May 5, the Irish Brigade marched down the Catharpin Road and then the Brock Road into the Wilderness towards Todd's Tavern. Although General Meagher had long left the brigade, his small arms concepts were still current in the New York and Pennsylvania regiments, armed with smoothbore muskets. The longer range Enfield rifle muskets carried by the 28th earned the Bay State Irishmen the dubious honor and "arduous duties" of serving as flankers in the dense undergrowth on either side of the brigade column.[8]

General Lee felt his best chance against the numerically superior Army of the Potomac was to strike the Yankees while they were passing though the Wilderness. The confident Confederate commander began to concentrate his army, fully expecting a reprise of Chancellorsville on the same terrain.

Elements of Major General Gouvenor K. Warren's V Corps encountered the enemy and attacked them on the morning of May 5. Initially successful, the V Corps advance came unhinged when the Rebels counter-attacked in the tangled forest. Other Federal forces, including elements of the VI and II Corps, fended off enemy attacks on the Yankee left flank, which was anchored along the Brock Road further south.

General Barlow's First Division arrived on the scene around 5:00 PM and threw up rudimentary breastworks from whatever materials were at hand, including felled rotten trees, along the Brock Road. Shortly afterward, Barlow ordered Colonel Nelson A. Miles' First Brigade and Colonel Smyth's Irish Brigade into the fight. With skirmishers from the the 28th Massachusetts out front, the two Yankee outfits formed in line of battle around 5:00 PM and moved off the Brock Road for about 300 yards into the woods. There they encountered Brigadier General James H. Lane's brigade of North Carolinians.

When the Massachusetts men ran into the main Rebel line, they fell back under a scattering fire to join the Irish Brigade's line of battle. As Captain James A. McIntire of the 28th reached the brigade lines he noticed one of his skirmishers lying wounded and ran back to rescue him. McIntire dragged the injured soldier towards the main line under an increasingly withering fire and then he too was hit – gutshot by a minie ball. The nineteen year old captain calmly walked a half mile to a hospital, where, later that evening, he died.

While the wounded straggled to the rear, the rest of Miles' and Smyth's men advanced firing until they overlapped the enemy on both flanks. The two Federal outfits routed Lane's Rebels and drive them back through a tangle of thorn bushes, vines, scrub oak and pitch pine until they hit another Rebel line. The fight then turned into a deadly slugging match that went on until dark.

As was his custom, Father Corby followed the Irish Brigade into action on horseback, ready to assist casualties. One of the first he saw, Private Daniel Lynch of the 88th, inspired him with more than the usual pity. The private, who lost a good job in the Quartermaster's Department due to "many blunders for want of system and education," had been returned to the ranks of his regiment at the outset of the campaign. Lynch, a "brave, dutiful soldier," was riddled with eight bullets and died in the Wilderness[9]

The Irishmen were relieved at dark, withdrew to the road and went to work improving their hasty field fortifications with leaves and dirt

Breastworks of Hancock's Corps on the Brock Road. (*Battles and Leaders*)

loosened by bayonets and scooped up by hand. The brigade was held in reserve the following morning when the rest of General Hancock's II Corps smashed into the Rebels deployed astride the Orange Plank Road. Initially successful, Hancock's assault was halted and driven back by General James Longstreet's Corps, which arrived just in time to save the Confederate army. The II Corps men rallied along the Brock Road line in the early afternoon as the enemy attack faltered, due at least in part to Longstreet's wounding by his own men.

    Shortly after 4:00 PM General Lee ordered a massive attack on the II Corps position. Thirteen brigades of Rebels stormed forward screaming and shooting and veterans would remember the ensuing half hour of musketry as some of the heaviest they ever experienced. The Irishmen had torn open cartridges and loaded their smoothbores with extra buckshot, and their volleys cut a vicious swath in the attackers. The Rebels were

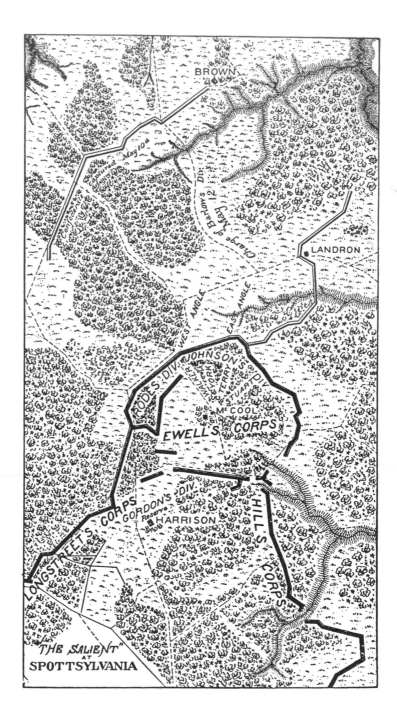

BROWN

Road May 10th

Barlow's Div.

Charge May 12

LANDRON

WEST ANGLE

EAST ANGLE

WALKER

YORK

STUART

TERRY'S DIV.

JOHNSON'S DIV.

RODES DIV.

M^c COOL

EWELL'S CORPS

GORDON'S DIV.

Reserv.

HARRISON

LONGSTREET'S CORPS

HILL'S CORPS

"THE SALIENT"
AT
SPOTTSYLVANIA

repulsed everywhere along the line except where the Yankee defenses were set afire, forcing the defenders to retreat temporarily. The men of the 116th fell back a hundred yards when burning paper from their buck and ball cartridges ignited the leaves piled atop their defensive berm. Some of the Pennsylvanians lost their knapsacks, which were leaning against the works, to the flames, before the Rebels were driven back.

The battle sputtered down to occasional rattles of musketry punctuated by the screams of wounded men burning to death in the smoke and fire swept underbrush. General Hancock collected his thoughts and tried to make sense of it all. One thing he remembered out of the chaos was that the "Irish Brigade...behaved with great steadiness and gallantry."[10]

Although as tactically stymied in the Wilderness as Hooker had been the year before, General Grant did not follow precedent and withdraw across the Rappahannock. Instead, the Federal commander moved the Union army southeast to Spotsylvania Courthouse in an attempt to hook around the Army of Northern Virginia's right flank. Unfortunately for the Yankees, the ever resourceful General Lee anticipated his opponent's move and Rebel infantry reached Spotsylvania in time to dig in and hold off the Yankees.

The Irish Brigade was one of the last Union units to march out of the Wilderness. On May 8, as Federal forward elements were sparring with the Rebels at Spotsylvania, the brigade marched down hot and dusty roads to Todd's Tavern, arriving there around 11:00 AM. After deploying the 63rd as skirmishers, Colonel Smyth pushed the brigade forward two miles before digging defensive earthworks. The Irishmen skirmished with the enemy that night and then moved on, shooting, digging and marching through May 11, as they slipped down the dirt roads towards Spotsylvania.

Following Colonel Emory Upton's successful penetration of the enemy lines at Spotsylvania with a ten regiment task force on May 10, General Grant reasoned that where a reinforced brigade might go and achieve temporary success, an Army Corps might follow and secure victory. Grant ordered General Hancock to lead his entire II Corps in a massive assault on "the Muleshoe," a salient in the Confederate line several hundred yards to the left of Upton's attack.

On the night of May 11, the II Corps marched from right to left across the army's rear, passing as quietly as possible through the camps of the VI Corps to the attack's jump off point. One soldier in the 28th Massachusetts remembered orders to "move cautious to the front." In the dark before dawn on May 12, Hancock's men swept forward in fog and drizzle across ditches and up and down swales towards the Rebels, who were dug in on high ground several hundred yards away. Red-orange dots from the muskets of a few fleeing Confederate pickets flickered like fireflys in the gloom ahead of the Yankees, Here and there a soldier dropped.[11]

The Irish Brigade attacked in the First Division's second line, but surged to the front when the division encountered the Rebel abatis, a thicket of cut down trees and brush spread in front of defensive works to hinder attackers. The Irishmen frantically tore through the abatis and rushed through an ill aimed volley from hastily awakened Confederates. Filled with battle frenzy, they swarmed over the Rebel line.

"We run this machine now," announced Private Henry J. "Blinkey" Bell of the 116th to the bleary eyed defenders of the Muleshoe as Lieutenant Peter H. Fraley of the Pennsylvania regiment ran a resisting Rebel through with his sword. Screaming, shooting, swinging and stabbing, the II Corps men wrecked Major General Edward "Allegheny" Johnson's division, and captured the bulk of it, including Johnson himself, who was reportedly taken in his tent by a private from the 28th Massachusetts.[12]

Flushed with victory, the somewhat disorganized Yankees rolled helter skelter into the Rebel rear, where they encountered a second enemy line manned by rapidly arriving reserves. Heavy fire halted the mob of Federals and a Confederate counterattack pushed them back to the point of their breakthrough. As the Rebels charged, the Irishmen and their Yankee comrades, still full of fight, rapidly prepared a defense. A Corporal O'Neil of the 63rd jumped on top of the captured breastworks and personally challenged the Graybacks: "We have licked you before you blankety blanked Rebs, and we can do it again. Come on! We are ready for you!" The Galway born corporal was answered with a bullet in the mouth. As he went to the rear, O'Neil brandished his fist and yelled through bloody broken teeth "I'll pay you for that some day!" The II Corps men stopped the enemy in a savage close range battle. The sanguinary struggle continued in a pouring rain all day and into the night, until the Rebels finally withdrew to their reserve line.[13]

Although the brigade's severe losses did not approach those suffered at Antietam or Fredericksburg, casualties were high in the fight for Spotsylvania's "Bloody Angle." Among the dead was "Blinkey" Bell of the 116th, one of the first men into the enemy lines, who was killed in the attack on the Rebel reserve position. Color Sergeant Peter Welsh of the 28th was hit in the arm in the attack's initial phases. What appeared to be a minor flesh wound became septic, most likely through a surgeon's probing, and Welsh died in Washington's Carver Hospital on May 28.

From May 13 through 17, the men of the brigade were constantly on the move, throwing up earthworks and skirmishing. During these maneuvers, Colonel Richard Byrnes of the 28th returned from recruiting duty in Massachusetts with a new green flag for his regiment. As the brigade's senior colonel, Byrnes replaced Colonel Smyth, who was transferred to the command of another brigade.

On the morning of May 18 the II Corps charged enemy fortifications once again. The Irish Brigade stormed across 200 yards of open ground towards the Rebel lines. Some soldiers got caught in the Rebel abatis and were killed while attempting to extricate themselves. Others made a lodgement in the rifle pits of the Confederate first line. Captain Blake of the 69th, attempting to lead his men on to the enemy's second line, climbed atop a rifle pit and urged his men on with fighting words. They were the last words he ever spoke.

The 69th's Lieutenant R. P. King, a Bull Run veteran, was shot in the throat. The twenty-five year old Kerry man died three days later. The lieutenant was not the first of his family to make the supreme sacrifice for his adopted country. King's brother, Lieutenant Timothy King of the 88th, had been killed in action at Fair Oaks, one of the first combat fatalities in the Irish Brigade.

Others were luckier. Although his comrades in the 116th initially thought part of Robert Glendenning's head was blown off by a shell that whooshed by, the round merely took off the private's toupee. Corporal Samuel Clear of the same regiment had his life saved by his belt plate. The plate had shifted from the front of Clear's body to the side, where it was hit by a minie ball which had already penetrated a ten round package of spare ammunition and a combination knife, fork and spoon utensil.

The 28th's advance came to a halt when the regiment's line was enfiladed. Pinned down by Rebel fire from front and side, the Massachusetts outfit lost Major Andrew J. Lawlor, Captain James Magner, Captain William Cochrane and eight enlisted men killed as well as a number of

Colonel Richard Byrnes, 28th Massachusetts. A regular army enlisted men for ten years prior to the outbreak of the Civil War, Byrnes rose to the rank of sergeant major of the 1st U. S. Cavalry. After the war began he was commissioned a lieutenant. Following his assumption of command, Colonel Byrnes shook up the 28th and introduced the regiment to regular army ways. Although his popularity in the 28th had its ups and downs, Byrnes' integrity and military abilities were never challenged. The Cavan born colonel was mortally wounded while leading the Irish Brigade at Cold Harbor (USAMHI)

officers and men wounded. That night the rest of the brigade withdrew, leaving the 116th behind on picket duty among the unburied dead.

The Irishmen broke camp on the night of May 20 then crossed the Mat River at Milford and marched to Guiney's Station the following day. On May 23, Byrne's brigade escorted supply and ammunition wagons and marched as rear guard for the II Corps.

The Army of the Potomac sidled southward in heat and dust and then driving rain to the banks of the North Anna River, which the Irish Brigade crossed on May 24. The Yankee army was checked again along the North Anna by fast marching Rebels who held the advantage of interior lines. Suffering from exhaustion, weather and short rations, the men of the Irish Brigade recrossed the river on the morning of May 25, marched three miles and then spent the rest of that day and all the next ripping up the railbed of the Richmond and Fredricksburg Railroad. The Irishmen laid rails across crosstie bonfires then watched the cherry red steel warp into uselessness. Their mission of destruction accomplished, they marched on to the Pamunkey and tramped across the river on a pontoon bridge.

The surviving veterans of the Irish Brigade – the hard bitten boys of '61 – now found themselves in familiar surroundings. On May 29, the bedraggled brigade arrived at Hazelbone's Tavern near the Old Gaines' Mill battlefield. Following a brief rest the Irishmen advanced three miles towards Totopotomoy Creek, passing a scattering of dead Rebel cavalrymen left behind by Major General Philip Sheridan's hard driving horse soldiers. Beyond the dead men, the Irish threw up breastworks and deployed pickets, who skirmished with the enemy.

On Tuesday, June 1, the II Corps left the Totopotomy line and marched towards Cold Harbor, where the rest of the Army of the Potomac had concentrated. Arriving on July 2, the brigade deployed facing the Rebels, with its right flank in an apple orchard. Some men climbed the trees to pick green apples, and drew sniper fire from observant enemy sharpshooters, Color Sergeant T. A. Sloan of the 116th had his coffee cup shot out of his hand. Another Pennsylvanian, Sergeant William Chambers, realized it was his birthday and humorously speculated on what present he might receive. A Rebel sniper gave him a bullet through the arm.

General Grant ordered a general attack on the Rebel lines for June 3. Late that day, three Union Corps, the II, VI and XVIII, assaulted what proved to be an impregnable position. The II corps attacked on the left, with the Irish Brigade in the second line of General Barlow's First Division.

Barlow's attack was initially successful. The First Division men seized an advanced portion of the Rebel line and captured several artillery pieces. As the division moved on the main enemy line, however, it was caught in murderous frontal and cross fires and was repulsed with heavy losses. Among the casualties was the severely wounded Colonel Byrnes. Byrnes was hit in the back by a minie ball which had already driven through the chest and arm of his aide, Captain James D. Brady of the 63rd. The bullet lodged near the colonel's spine. The thirty-one year old Byrnes, born in County Cavan, had risen through the prewar army ranks to sergeant major of the 1st U. S. Cavalry. His bravery as an Indian fighter and then a junior officer in the Peninsula campaign had earned him the command of the 28th. The same courage now cost Byrnes his life, as he died at Armory Square Hospital in Washington on June 12.[14]

Their commander down, Byrnes' men held the captured Rebel forward position until dark, then fell back to their original position. All of the Irish regiments were badly cut up; the experience of the 28th Massachusetts was typical. Captain James Fleming of the 28th reported that "our men fell in heaps." Although stragglers came in throughout the night the 28th initially fell back to its original position with but "3 lieutenants and 66 men for duty."[15]

Not all the brigade's casualties were physically wounded. The grueling campaign of 1864 cost the Irish Brigade more psychological casualties than it had ever suffered in the past. In the smokey hell of the Wilderness a Berdan's Sharpshooter saw a sergeant, who claimed he was from the 69th, shoot his own trigger finger off. Here, at Cold harbor, several officers, including Lieutenant Fraley of the 116th, who had been one of "the bravest of the brave" and led the May 12 charge at Spotsylvania, cracked under the stress of constant combat. Fraley's regimental commander remembered that the lieutenant's "mind gave way." He was discharged on a surgeon's certificate.[16]

The survivors fought on under the command of Colonel Patrick Kelly, who had led them north to Gettysburg. Through June 11 the brigade was engaged in picket duty and digging entrenchments at Cold Harbor under constant fire from shells and snipers. The Irishmen finally marched away from the Cold Harbor killing ground during the night of

June 12, as Grant stole a march on Lee. The Union commander hoped to capture Petersburg, a vital rail center south of Richmond, before the Rebels could react. Kelly and his decimated Irish Brigade were ready to do their part.

Model 1858 forage cap, size 3 (modern 7) manufactured by L. J. & I. Phillips. Writing, in ink, on the label inside identifies the cap as the property of "Sergt. Henry McQuade 69th NYV." The twenty year old McQuade enlisted in Company D of the 69th Volunteers in Chicago as a corporal in 1861. He was subsequently promoted to sergeant and first sergeant and wounded at Fredericksburg. McQuade was mustered out when the regiment was consolidated into two companies in 1863 but returned to duty as a second lieutenant in Company C on January 28, 1864. Wounded again on August 14, 1864, McQuade was one of the officers captured in the Rebel picket raid in November. After his exchange in February, 1865, he was mustered in as Captain, Company H, and was mustered out with that rank. The numbers on the cap are from the post Civil War period and appear to have been placed on the cap by McQuade following the war. (Martin L. Schoenfeld Collection)

Chapter 6

"Veteran Soldiers Wept Like Children"

T he battle weary soldiers of the Irish Brigade crossed the Chickahominy, the first river the brigade had crossed to go into battle two years before, on June 13, 1864, and then marched to the James, where they threw up breastworks at Wilcox's Landing. There the Irishmen were able to rest for a day, wash their clothes and bodies and catch some fish to supplement their salt pork and hardtack diet. The following day they crossed the James at Windmill Point and went into camp on the south bank of the river.

On June 15 the II Corps moved on to Petersburg, arriving there, after an exhausting march, at midnight. The Irish had outmarched their supplies but the black soldiers of Brigadier General Edward W. Hinks' Division, who had mounted a successful attack earlier that day, shared their own rations with the famished Hibernians. "Never did the army cracker and raw salt pork taste so sweet," one soldier remembered.[1]

Although Grant beat Lee to Petersburg, XVIII Corps commander Major General William F. "Baldy" Smith's dawdling squandered a golden opportunity. Unaccountably, Smith halted his advance after his men had overrun the outer defenses of Petersburg, allowing Confederate forces to arrive in time to save the "Cockade City."

The issue was still in some doubt, however, when the Irish Brigade was thrown into the attack on the evening of June 16. The Irishmen overran several earthwork forts, and held them under heavy enemy fire until they were relieved at 9:00 PM. The brigade was badly shot up, however, and among the casualties was Colonel Kelly, who was killed in action. With the death of Galway born Kelly, a well loved commander who

113

had served as a captain in the 69th Militia at Bull Run, "strong old veteran soldiers wept like children, and wrung their hands in frenzy." Once more the Irish Brigade, with more dead men than living on its rolls, appeared to be on the verge of extinction. One veteran despaired that the unit "was a Brigade no longer" and that nothing remained but "the recollection of its services and sufferings."[2]

The brigade, now under the command of Major Richard Moroney of the 69th, a veteran of the Mexican War and the 69th Militia, spent the rest of June marching, digging and skirmishing around Petersburg. Although severely understrength, the Irish regiments still mustered their share of tough customers. One of these, Private Michael DeLacy of the 63rd, called out: "Say Johnnies? You are a low lived lot of spalpeens. You face the Yankees in the open and we'll knock the devil out of yees. We can lick yees every time." DeLacey's taunts led to a temporary truce and a between the lines one on one bayonet duel with a Rebel. The Irish private dodged his opponent's thrust, clipped him in the chin with his musket butt and pinned the Reb to the ground with his foot. DeLacey, generous in victory, released his defeated enemy to a cheer from both lines. The private "after that day was borne on the rolls as 'Sergeant' DeLacey, an honor he honestly and bravely won."[3]

With the bulk of the Army of Northern Virginia now in the Petersburg defenses, General Grant abandoned frontal assaults and ordered Meade's Army of the Potomac to initiate a series of operations to extend the Federal lines towards the Confederate right flank. These Union moves threatened the vital rail and road communications connecting Petersburg with the rest of the South. The loss of these arteries would make the city, and Richmond as well, untenable.

Meade chose the II Corps, which had never lost a flag or artillery piece to the enemy, as his spearhead outfit. The corps, which had suffered massive casualties in the drive south from the Rapidan, was, however, no longer the unit it used to be. The Rebels, their backs against the wall, responded savagely to the maneuvers of General Hancock's men.

On June 22, Confederate Brigadier General William Mahone launched a surprise attack on the II Corps' left flank, which was deployed along the Jerusalem Plank Road near Johnston's Farm. The Irish Brigade, especially the 116th Pennsylvania, suffered especially heavy losses in Mahone's attack. After the fight, Sam Clear, now acting first sergeant of the 116th's Company K, counted eight men still in ranks out of the eighty-seven who had crossed the Rapidan on May 3. The 63rd New York lost twenty-five men wounded and missing. When the day was done, the II Corps could no longer boast it had never lost a color or gun.

At the end of June the Irish Brigade, along with other long service II Corps brigades, was broken up and its decimated regiments reassigned in an attempt to balance brigade strength in the corps, an act that gave rise to much righteous indignation in the ranks. The three veteran New York regiments remained together under the overall command of Major Moroney, and then Major John W. Byron, as part of the new "Consolidated Brigade" along with six other First Division Empire State outfits.

The 28th Massachusetts was assigned to the Second Division's First Brigade and the 116th Pennsylvania to the division's Fourth Brigade. The men of the 116th, although primarily American born soldiers of mixed ethnic backgrounds, genuinely regretted leaving the Irish Brigade. One advantage did accrue with the transfer, however. The Pennsylvanians turned in their standard Irish Brigade issue smoothbore muskets: "It was a welcome change, for while the old weapon with the buck and ball was an excellent one at close quarters, the men felt that the new rifle piece was far superior, especially on the skirmish line."[4]

On July 26 the Consolidated Brigade broke camp and crossed the James River, then marched towards the Richmond front occupied by the Army of the James as part of a feint to distract attention from the explosion of the Petersburg mine. The brigade arrived at Deep Bottom at 4:00 AM the following morning and supported the First Division's First Brigade in a July 28 attack on the enemy lines. The Irishmen remained at Deep Bottom until July 29, when they headed back to Petersburg, arriving there on July 30.

The Consolidated Brigade camped at Petersburg until August 12, then marched to City Point, boarded troop transports and returned to Deep Bottom. On August 14, the Irishmen were ordered to probe the enemy positions. Major Byron led the 88th in a bayonet assault into a woodlot occupied by Confederate skirmishers and succeeded in driving the Rebels back and capturing their rifle pits. Shortly afterward the brigade returned to Petersburg.

On August 22 and 23, the Irishmen, as part of yet another II Corps advance on the Confederate supply lines below Petersburg, advanced down

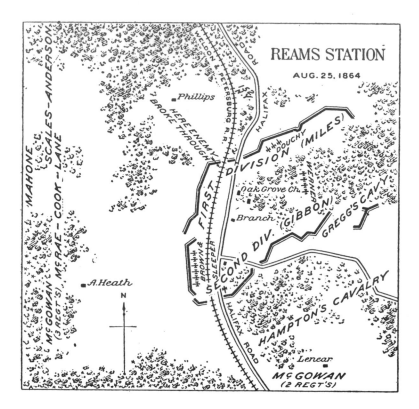

REAMS STATION

AUG. 25, 1864

the Weldon Railroad beyond Reams' Station, tearing up track as they went. When Rebel troops moved out of their defenses and threatened the Federal advance, Brigadier General Nelson A. Miles' First and Brigadier General John Gibbon's Second Divisions fell back on Reams' Station and took up a defensive position in an old horseshoe shaped entrenchment.

The Consolidated Brigade's line ran parallel to the railroad, with a slashed timber abatis to the front. The entire position was poorly sited and easy for the enemy to enfilade. To make matters worse, fire at the defenders of one leg of the horseshoe was liable to hit the defenders of the other side in the back.

The horseshoe was also too long a line to properly defend with the number of troops available. After deploying sufficient skirmishers beyond the earthworks to the front, the Consolidated Brigade line, which should have been held by two ranks of men shoulder to shoulder, was manned by a thin screen of soldiers a pace apart. Still, the Irishmen's deadly volleys shattered several enemy advances. Pinned down by musketry, some Rebels raised their hands in surrender and came into the Irish lines.

All did not go as well elsewhere, however. When a slashing Confederate charge penetrated General Gibbon's Second Division, Rebels swarmed into the Yankee rear. The Irishmen leaped over the defensive berm ready to fight the enemy now behind them, only to be overrun by another wave of Graybacks coming at their position from the front.

A number of men from the Irish Brigade regiments, including Major Byron, Captain Maurice Wall of the 69th and Lieutenant Grainger, the Antietam sharpshooter of the 88th, were captured. The 69th lost six officers and men wounded and forty-five missing, most of the latter prisoners. Reams' Station was an unmitigated disaster for the Army of the Potomac's grand old II Corps, now nothing but a burnt out ghost of its former self. The fortunes of the corps, as well as the fragmented Irish Brigade, had reached their nadir.

Irish Brigade soldiers provided one bright spot for the Union during the day's fighting, however. Captain Benjamin of the 63rd, commanding the Consolidated Brigade skirmish line, was cut off by the rapid Rebel advance. Benjamin and his men cooly evaded capture and rescued several Yankee prisoners from their captors as they worked their way back to the main Union line.

As always, the indomitable Irishmen bounced back. Replacements arrived and wounded men returned to duty in the weeks following Reams' Station. On September 4, the New York regiments were joined by the men of the 28th Massachusetts in a celebration commemorating the third anniversary of the founding of the Irish Brigade. General Meagher, who had spent the last year and a half on the lecture circuit and was now seeking a new military assignment, attended the festivities.

The brigade's anniversary ceremonies began with a solemn High Mass co-celebrated by Fathers Corby and Ouellet, followed by a "collation of sorts in 'Bowery Hall'" attended by distinguished military guests, including Generals Meade, Hancock and Miles. Then, in his own inimitable way, General Meagher addressed the men of the brigade, drawn up in front of him in "close column." To wild cheers, Meagher reminded the

Colonel Robert Nugent, Colonel of the 69th NYSV and last commander of the Irish Brigade. Nugent, from Kilkeel in County Down, served in the 69th Militia as well as the 69th New York Volunteer Infantry and also, after the outbreak of the war, held a commission as a captain in the U. S. regular army. He received the brevet (honorary) rank of brigadier general. (Roger D. Hunt Collection)

men of his old command that: "Every battle field, from Bull Run to Reams' Station, but added another laurel to the wreath which the war would transfer for them to posterity."[5]

Other generals testified to the constancy of the Irishmen. General Miles, their Division commander, bore "testimony to the unflinching bravery of the Irish troops on all occasions," taking care to publicly note that the brigade's regiments were in no way responsible for the Reams' Station disaster.[6]

As the generals spoke, the Irish Brigade was rising once more from its ashes. Replacements continued to arrive fron New York, and, on October 22, General Miles requested that the Consolidated Brigade be disbanded and its regiments restored to their original organizations. On November 1, 1864, the three New York Irish regiments, mustering a total of 856 enlisted men, once more became the Second Brigade of the First Division of the II Corps. Within a week, the Irishmen of the 28th Massachusetts returned to the brigade.

The Irish Brigade's new commander was an old friend, Colonel Robert Nugent. In announcing his assumption of command, Nugent evoked the brigade's memory of the glory days of 1862, when the outfit was one of the finest military organizations that ever was – or would be. Said Nugent: "Never has a regimental color of that organization [the Irish Brigade] graced the halls of its enemies. Let the spirit that animates the officers and men of the present be that which shall strive to emulate the deeds of the old brigade."[7]

In November the men of the 88th New York presented their regimental commander, Lieutenant Colonel Denis F. Burke, with "a magnificent steed and suitable equipments." First Sergeant Patrick J. Healy of Company E presented the horse and delivered the address. Healy recalled that Burke, like many of the brigade's officers, began his military career with the 69th Militia, cited his steadfast and heroic conduct in the years that followed, then handed him the reins of "Antietam." Burke, a Cork man, responded that it was his "proudest boast that I commanded the 88th from Gettysburg to Petersburg, and that they always maintained, whether on the march, in camp, or in the heat of battle, that obedience, fidelity and alacrity which ever distinguishes the Irish soldier." The colonel, no doubt a Fenian, added that he looked forward to the day when he

119

could "lead the remnant of the 88th to share in striking a stunning blow for the freedom of our dear old mother land."[8]

In the fall the regiments of the Irish Brigade discharged the veterans who had not reenlisted and received a new infusion of replacements: a mixture of draftees, substitutes for draftees and volunteer recruits. These men had no "basic training" like that provided to replacements in future wars, and were expected to learn the art of soldiering from the receiving units, which were often under enemy fire when the recruits joined them. Unfortunately, some of these new soldiers were poor military material. How poor, the brigade would soon find out.

In the waning days of 1864 an incident occurred which shocked the Irish Brigade veterans, particularly those of the proud 69th New York. The regiment was stationed along the Petersburg trench lines near Fort Davis. Perhaps in retaliation for a successful (but costly) trench raid led by hard fighting Lieutenant Colonel Burke of the 88th on October 29, the Rebels raided the Irish Brigade picket line on the night of October 30. The line, which ran between the opposing entrenched lines, was composed of posts about twenty yards apart connected by trenches. That night the positions were manned by two officers, three sergeants who were "acting lieutenants," and 230 enlisted men, 190 of whom were recent recruits.

Posing as a picket relief, Confederates infiltrated the left wing of the 69th's picket line and drive down it and the line of the neighboring 111th New York, scooping up prisoners as they went. The 111th lost 246 men captured, the 69th 168, including a lieutenant and all three acting lieutenants. Another party of Rebels approached the right wing of the 69th's line, commanded by veteran Lieutenant Murtha Murphy. The quick thinking Murphy ordered his men to fire, dispersing the raiders. When the lieutenant, who was slightly wounded in the head by a scattered return fire, was informed by a Third Division officer that the pickets along the line to his left "were either captured or had run away, leaving their muskets behind them in the trenches," he obliqued his command's left to protect that flank until he was relieved.[9]

The 69th lost the services of several valuable veterans who were captured in the incident. Among them was Waterford born Thomas McGrath, who had risen through the regiment's ranks from private to sergeant. An exemplar of the veteran soldiers who still served in the Irish Brigade, McGrath enlisted in 1861 and was wounded at Malvern Hill,

Fredericksburg, Gettysburg and Spotsylvania. While a prisoner at Richmond and then Salisbury, North Carolina, Sergeant McGrath would lead three escape attempts.[10]

An after action assessment of the affair led to the conclusion that ten of the 69th's recent recruits who had deserted to the enemy informed the Rebels of the picket line dispositions. General Miles, who had a good deal of respect for the Irish Brigade's military skills, opined that "the deserters from the Sixty Ninth New York were Rebels...." Some deserters were caught and suffered the ultimate punishment. Among these was the 69th's Private John Nicholas, a Canadian farmer who enlisted as a substitute for a New York draftee and joined the regiment in September. Recaptured following his desertion, Nicholas was executed March 10, 1865.[11]

On December 7 the Irish Brigade, which now included the 7th New York Heavy Artillery, moved to Hatcher's Run and was deployed in support of yet another advance on the Rebel lines of communications. Although Dixie was clearly on its way down, two of the 69th's recent replacements deserted off the picket line to the enemy on December 10. Following the Hatcher's Run operation the Irishmen marched back to Petersburg and spent the next month and a half in the trenches. On February 5, the brigade, now about 1,600 men strong, marched back to Hatcher's Run and threw up entrenchments under sporadic fire. This time the 69th played turnabout, as a number of Rebel deserters came into the brigade lines.

Although the Irish Brigade had been reconstituted, the 63rd and the 88th, at least, were still considerably understrength. "Look Out Bob" of the 63rd wrote home requesting that his regiment and the 88th be brought to full strength before the active campaign season. Bob lyrically argued that "surely the times do not admonish us to send the green flags back to the dusty archives at Albany, where the mice can play upon their harps."[12]

In March the Irish Brigade celebrated its last Saint Patrick's Day in the army. Although a visitor to the brigade found it "an affecting thing to see that handful of earnest Irish heroes, the remains of many terrible campaigns, casting aside the drilled sedateness of the soldier," the festivities proved not nearly as wild as in previous years.[13]

As usual, the day began with a High Mass, celebrated by Father Ouellet. The brigade's distinguished guests, including General Meade and

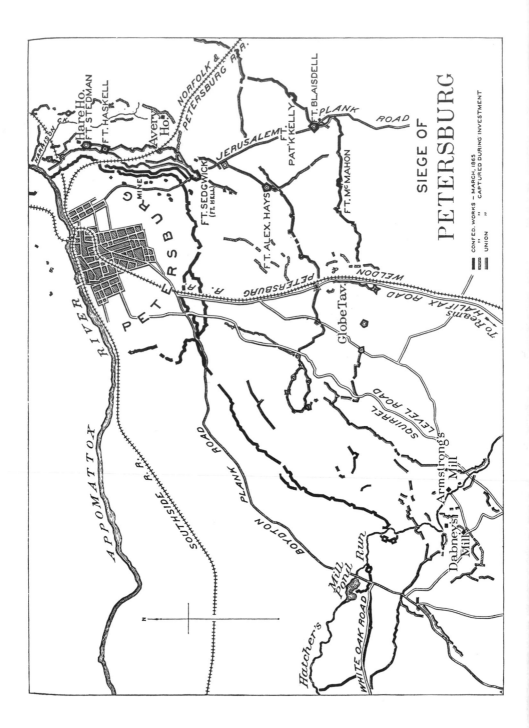

SIEGE OF

PETERSBURG

CONFED. WORKS – MARCH, 1865
" " CAPTURED DURING INVESTMENT
UNION "

NORFOLK & PETERSBURG R.R.

PLANK ROAD

FT. BLAISDELL

HareHo.
FT. STEDMAN
FT. HASKELL
Avery Ho.
HARRISON
CA.

JERUSALEM

FT. PAT'K KELLY

FT. McMAHON

FT. SEDGWICK
(FT. HELL)

FT. ALEX. HAYS

MINE

P E T E R S B U R G

PETERSBURG R.R.

GlobeTav.

WELDON

HALIFAX ROAD

To Ream's

LEVEL ROAD

SQUIRREL ROAD

APPOMATTOX RIVER

SOUTHSIDE R.R.

PLANK ROAD

BOYDTON

Armstrongs Mill

Dabney's Mill

Mill Pond Run

Hatcher's

WHITE OAK ROAD

122

a dozen Division and Corps Commanders, enjoyed the by now traditional officers' steeple chase, as well as a "flat race." When all was said and done, several thousand dollars changed hands among the wagering officers. Second Lieutenant Michael McConville of the 69th, who had survived almost four years of war, fell from his horse during the steeple chase and fractured his skull. The lieutenant died of his injuries more than a week later.

Although the mule race was dropped, the enlisted men still competed in sack and foot races, both of which were won by a "dashing Celt" from the 88th, who pocketed around forty dollars per race. An officer deeply regretted that army regulations did not allow the enlisted men whiskey "wherewith to drown their shamrocks." By previous years' standards the officers and honored guests did not fare so well either, and had to make do with "little more than a snack at a sandwich, washed down by commissary whiskey," the latter supplied free of charge by the commissary of the 28th Massachusetts. Background music for the festivities was provided by the band of the First Division, II Corps, under the leadership of a Mr. Higgins of Boston.[14]

On March 25, 1865, the Rebellion began to gasp its last. General Lee launched a desperate assault on Fort Stedman in the IX Corps area on the Federal right flank. Although the fort fell in the initial assault, a Yankee counterattack drove the Rebels back to their own lines with heavy losses. As part of the Union response to the Fort Stedman affair, the Irish Brigade advanced on Skinner's Farm near Hatcher's Run and was soon engaged in a stand-up fight which lasted several hours.

The Irish Brigade of March, 1865 was, on the face of it, an entirely different outfit than the Irish Brigade that first marched out of Camp California in the long ago. A small but splendid core of officers and men nurtured the spiritual flame that originally ignited the brigade's soul, however. At Skinner's Farm that flame rose high and the Irishmen provided a "splendid spectacle of unflinching bravery" for all who watched. Among the keepers of the flame was Captain John D. Mulhall of the 69th, who moved out in front of the skirmish line to inspire his men. When the Rebels tried to outflank his line, Mulhall, a Roscommon man and a veteran of the Papal Brigade, wheeled his command by an oblique movement to confront them and was hit by a minie ball that smashed his leg. The captain, who had returned to action after recovering from a Cold

Harbor wound, laid on the battlefield for two hours before he received medical attention.

The 28th Massachusetts, now reduced to a five company battalion, shot up all its ammunition and lost a large number of officers and men killed and wounded, including the unit's commander, Lieutenant Colonel James Flemming, who was hit in the shoulder. The 4th New York Heavy Artillery, which had replaced the 7th in the brigade, suffered a number of casualties as well.

On March 29 General Miles' First Division marched in support of the V Corps and the Army of the Potomac's cavalry, all under the command of Major General Philip Sheridan, in the final Union move on the Confederate lines of communication. The Yankees crossed the Boydton Plank Road and then the White Road, driving for the Confederate rear. Sheridan fought and beat the Rebels at Five Forks and then the Union VI Corps broke through the Confederate lines in front of Petersburg itself. General Lee realized the time had come to quit the Cockade City – and Richmond as well.

On April 2, 1865, the day the VI Corps broke the enemy lines, the Irish Brigade advanced on Sutherland Station, and when the Rebels abandoned Petersburg the following day, the II Corps, now led by Major General Andrew A. Humphreys, joined in the arduous pursuit. The Irish Brigade marched hard after the enemy, constantly skirmishing with the Confederate rear guard.

The Rebel army leaked a constant stream of prisoners, supply wagons and cannons. The Confederates attempted stands here and there, most notably at Sailor's Creek, where they were overrun by a blue tide. On April 7, the Irish Brigade engaged in a sustained skirmish with the Rebels near Farmville. That evening General Miles and Brigadier General Seth Williams, adjutant general of the Army of the Potomac, arrived at the brigade's line with a flag of truce. When the shooting stopped Colonel Nugent and his aide, Captain John Oldershaw, accompanied Miles and Williams through the Irish picket lines to deliver General Grant's initial surrender demand to General Lee.

The following morning the Rebels were gone. The Irishmen took up the pursuit at 5:30 AM and followed the enemy towards Appomattox Court House at a grueling pace, men falling out from exhaustion all along the road. The II Corps caught up with the Confederates, now ringed by other Union forces, at midday on April 9. General Humphreys began to deploy his corps to attack, but halted when Rebel officers informed him that surrender negotiations were in progress. At 4:00 PM the men of the II Corps received word that General Lee had capitulated.

This, the brigade's last campaign, was not without loss. The 28th Massachusetts suffered "six commissioned officers wounded, eleven enlisted men killed and sixty-six wounded out of a total of a hundred eighty-four with which it started at the commencement of the campaign." The 63rd New York lost one man killed and five wounded, the 69th three killed and five wounded and the 88th four killed and twelve wounded.[15]

Although General Joseph Johnston's army was still in the field and some Confederate holdouts in the west fought on into the summer, Lee's surrender effectively ended the Civil War. It certainly ended the Irish Brigade's war, some four years after the militiamen of the 69th New York were electrified by the news that Fort Sumter had been fired on. On April 11 the men of the II Corps marched away from Appomattox to Burkesville, Virginia, where they camped until April 30. On May 2, the corps and the Irish Brigade began their long trek home. The brigade marched through Jetersville and Amelia Court House to Richmond, then through Hanover Court House to Fredericksburg, and then on to Alexandria, where the Army of the Potomac cleaned its uniforms, burnished its brass and weapons and prepared itself for one more march.

On May 22, 1865, thousands of civilians crowded into the capital for the Army of the Potomac's last review – the "Grand Review." It had rained for a few days, but May 22 dawned cloudless and sunny. The civilians lined Pennsylvania Avenue and broke into cheers and thunderous applause as the sun bronzed veterans of famous units swung down the street. At 2:00 PM Colonel Nugent, astride a smartly prancing black horse, led the Irish Brigade, its green flags and stars and stripes snapping in the spring breeze, past the reviewing stand. As at Fredericksburg, the scene of the brigade's greatest and most heroic disaster, each veteran proudly bore a sprig of boxwood in his hat.

There was nothing left now but the return home. Captain Maurice Wall led the first detachment, 200 convalescents and freed POWs from the 63rd, 69th and 88th, back to New York. Wall's men were paid and mustered out of the service on Hart's Island in late June.

The core of the old Irish Brigade, the 63rd, 69th and 88th New

"Return of the Flags of the Irish Brigade" by Thomas Waterman Wood. The bullet riddled Irish colors return to New York City. (West Point Museum)

York Volunteer Infantry and the 28th Massachusetts Volunteer Infantry, less the convalescents who had preceded them and recent recruits who were transferred to other outfits for another few weeks service, arrived at Manhattan's Battery Barracks on July 2 and were escorted by the First Division of the New York State National Guard through the city on July 4. The veteran Irishmen, 700 strong, "every one of whom looked strong and hearty; their faces, bronzed by the exposures of the field were, along the march, wreathed with smiles, as cheer after cheer rent the air, welcoming them back to citizenship and their former homes."[16]

Following the parade the Bay State boys of the 28th pushed on to Boston, where they were mustered out later in the week. The New York veterans, some 400 strong, marched to Irving Hall and "gave three cheers for their commanders and 'three for Gen. Meagher, the man who raised the Irish Brigade.'" Meagher's address to the survivors of this little band of brothers, although uncharacteristically brief, was effective, especially when he spoke of the brigade's dead. Meagher's call for "a round tower with a cathedral, like that of former times, to commemorate what they have done," drew thunderous applause. And then Brevet Brigadier General Nugent brought them to attention and marched them out of the hall and into the rest of their lives – and history.[17]

Monument to the Irish Brigade's New York outfits on the rocky hill beyond the wheatfield where the brigade fought July 2, 1863. the monument was dedicated in 1888. (Bill Goble)

Epilogue
"Where Are the Others"

There is no round tower, nor is there a cathedral. As with many things Thomas Francis Meagher envisioned, they did not come to pass. There are instead forgotten mass graves and forgotten single ones, marked and unmarked, stretching from the Peninsula of Virginia to Calvary Cemetery in New York and beyond.

For a time it appeared there might be nothing at all but the graves to remember them by. Then, on July 2, 1888, they came back to Gettysburg. They were middle aged men now, and some older than that. They gathered not on the field of their greatest fight, but America's. They walked the Wheatfield once again, and up the Stony Hill, where their blast of buck and ball and flashing bayonets had swept away the Carolinians. Then they walked back through the Wheatfield where they were caught in the crossfire during the retreat and where "Jersey" Gallagher of the 116th went down with five bullets in him and so many others fell to the deadly Rebel musketry. They set up an organ by the rock from which Father Corby had granted absolution, and Grace Haverty, the brigade quartermaster's daughter, played "Tenting Tonight." And there wasn't a dry eye to be found.

Father Corby himself had been busy since he left the army. His duties as president of the expanding College of Notre Dame had overshadowed his wartime experiences and he had lost contact with his old comrades in arms. In 1888, however, he, like almost 50,000 other veterans, was inexorably drawn to Gettysburg where he remembered the days when he too, was a soldier once and young. It was a Pauline experience for Corby and led to his own memoirs of the war and activity in veterans' affairs for the rest of his life.

When they dedicated the Irish Brigade monument at Gettysburg that July, Fathers Corby and Ouellet said mass and Corby delivered the homily. The veteran priest scanned the faces of the aging warriors before him, and then he said: "Here is what is left of us; where are the others?" And then he could speak no more, for memories of the others came flooding back and choked him with emotion.[1]

Now, as the twentieth century rushes to a close, it is perhaps time

Postwar medals of Lieutenant Thomas McGrath, 69th New York. (l. to r.) Civil War Campaign Medal; GAR Medal; Dedication of State Monuments at Gettysburg, July 1, 2, 3, "New York Day," Gettysburg Veteran Medal. (Thomas and Janice Clancy)

to remember those Irish Americans of the nineteenth – those who came to Gettysburg in 1888 – and "the others." It is time to remember James Haggerty slipping from the saddle and life at Bull Run, James Quinlan of Clonmel leading the 88th's charge on the guns on the peninsula for a medal of honor, blood spattered Peter Rafferty refusing to leave his comrades on the firing line at Malvern Hill, Pat Clooney limping with a flagstaff crutch on to death and glory at Antietam's Sunken Road, John Sheridan crawling through the maelstrom of Fredericksburg with a wounded private on his back, Color Sergeant Peter Welsh of the 28th, whose "million dollar wound" in the smokey hell of the Wilderness led to a totally unexpected death, Michael DeLacy, who turned an opportune vertical butt stroke into a sergeantcy at Petersburg, and Thomas Francis Meagher, who, although not without fault, became the embodiment of his brigade and, in some sense, of all Irishmen become Americans – and all "the others."

At Gettysburg, atop the stony hill where they fought, and where they came that day in 1888 stands the monument to what the 63rd and the 69th and the 88th New York Infantry and the scattered gunners of the old 2nd New York Artillery Battalion did there and, perforce, did elsewhere. With its tall, striking Celtic cross and the recumbent wolfhound at its base, the brigade monument stands not just for those few hundred New York men who fought on a little ridge for fifteen minutes on a hot bloody day in July, 1863. It stands for the men of the 28th Massachusetts and of the 116th Pennsylvania and of all the other regiments and soldiers, "Yankee" and Irish, who fought with the Irish Brigade and in all the armies of the Union. Most of all it stands for a country, that, far from perfect, took in others who were far from perfect themselves, and, in the process, became, to most of them, the last best hope of mankind.

One of the last surviving veterans of the Irish Brigade at Memorial Day ceremonies in New York in the 1930s. His GAR hat is adorned with evergreen, in commemoration of the sprigs of box elder worn by the men of the brigade at Fredericksburg and in the Grand Review in 1865. (From "Echos of the Blue & Gray," courtesy Bill Styple)

Recessional
"The Work is Finished"

On the occasion of the dedication of the 69th Regiment, New York National Guard's new armory on October 13, 1906, Lieutenant Colonel James J. Smith of the 69th New York Volunteers returned several Irish Brigade colors, which had remained in the hands of the brigade's veterans since the war, to the regiment which gave birth to the brigade. Smith's address at the presentation confirmed the historic and continuing links between the 69th New York National Guard, formerly the 69th New York State Militia, and the Irish Brigade.

The colonel's closing words evoked an image of the remnants of that once mighty brigade preparing to pass down history's highway to join those it left on the Peninsula, and at Antietam, Fredricksburg, Gettysburg, the Wilderness, Spotsylvania, Cold Harbor, Petersburg and a dozen dusty, ghostly crossroads in between:

"As I look on the large assemblage of soldiery, officers and men, my thoughts wander back for years to the remembrance of my loved, dead companions of the old Regiment and the Brigade, and, though their forms are not perceptible to mortal eye, I feel that their spirit forms are here assembled. I fancy that I look upon the forms of Corcoran, Meagher, Nugent, Haggerty, Kelly, McMahon and Murphy, and all that brave and daring few, and I judge from their benign mien and appearance that our action here to-day meets with their approval, and the attitude they assume seems to imply that they shed a benediction on the work we have done, and as the work is finished so the loved forms dissolve and disappear to return to their silent tents on Fame's Eternal Camping Ground - there to rest - yes my Comrades, in the words of the poet soldier O'Hara we will say:

Rest on, embalmed and sainted dead,
  Dear as the blood you gave;
No impious footsteps here shall tread
  The herbage on your grave;

Nor shall your glory be forgot
  While Fame her record keeps,
Or Honor points the hallowed spot
  Where Valor proudly sleeps.[1]

133

Commemorative tablet at Thomas Francis Meagher's birthplace, now the Granville Hotel on Meagher Quay on the Suir River, Waterford, Republic of Ireland (Joseph Bilby)

Appendix I
Meagher of the Sword

Paradoxically, the man often spoke with an upper class British accent, no doubt acquired at Stonyhurst College in Lancashire, where his Jesuit education, begun at Clongowes Wood in Ireland, was polished and completed. He could always summon a Waterford brogue when the occasion demanded, however.

Thomas Francis Meagher was born in Waterford on August 3, 1823, the son of a prosperous merchant. The discovery of Daniel O'Connell's speeches on Catholic Emancipation, coupled with a visit to recently independent Belgium in 1842, convinced Meagher that Ireland's only hope lay in independence from Britain.

This belief led him to O'Connell, who was then organizing massive public rallies in an attempt to force repeal of the Act of Union with Great Britain, which had abolished the Irish Parliament in 1800. Apprehensive about these gatherings, the government banned what would have been the largest of them, at Clontarf, in October, 1843. O'Connell, determined to avoid violence, declined to pursue his goals beyond the limits of the law and ended his campaign.

Insistence on legality lost O'Connell the support of the "Young Ireland" movement of Thomas Davis, Charles Gavan Duffy and John B. Dillon. Meagher, then a Dublin law student, shifted his allegiance to these more aggressive patriots and, in a speech stressing the legitimacy of violent opposition to oppression, earned the sobriquet "Meagher of the Sword."

Implicated in the rebellion conspiracy of 1848 which culminated in the somewhat ludicrous affray at the Widow McCormack's in Ballingary, Meagher, along with other leaders, was sentenced to death. He was, however, pardoned, and exiled to Tasmania, where he married Catherine Bennett before he escaped to America in 1852. There he became an instant celebrity and a symbol of the Irish fight for freedom.

Meagher traveled the lecture circuit, edited the New York *Irish News*, engaged in business travels to Central America and was admitted to the bar in New York. After the death of his wife, he married Elizabeth Townsend, the daughter of a wealthy New Yorker who was appalled to see

135

her convert to Catholicism and marry an Irishman, no matter how handsome or eloquent.

When the Civil War came, Thomas Francis Meagher was well integrated into Irish American and American politics and society. As the secession crisis heated up, he publicly expressed sympathy with the southern states. Following the firing on Fort Sumter, however, Meagher abruptly changed his opinion. This sudden about face startled and angered a number of people, particularly southerners.

While he still carried a verbal cudgel against the British and wore his ethnic identification proudly, Meagher was not a Fenian at the outset of the war. In 1886, when the general was long dead and unable to dispute the claim, John O'Mahoney, a former "young Irelander" and founding member of the Fenian movement, claimed that he had initiated Meagher into the Brotherhood on July 11, 1863. If so, it seems peculiar that O'Mahoney would write in 1864 that Meagher and other leaders of the Young Ireland movement would have "nothing to do with Fenianism."[1]

Meagher fell out of favor with other Irishmen besides Fenians. Some, both in the United States and back in Ireland, characterized the general as a military incompetent who needlessly sacrificed his men in battle and was careless about their welfare in camp. The general had to defend himself against such allegations as early as his return to New York on recruiting duty from the Peninsula in the summer of 1862. Others spread absurd rumors of Meagher's complicity with various unnamed "Yankees" bent on Irish Catholic genocide or denounced him as an opportunist who used the cause of Irish liberation to recruit soldiers for the Union and advance his own American political career. The horrendous casualties the Irish Brigade suffered at Antietam and Fredericksburg added fuel to these fires. Although praising Meagher as "a gentleman and a soldier," one of his own sergeants asserted that "he [Meagher] wanted to gain so much praise he would not spare his men."[2]

Unfortunately, Meagher himself may have contributed to allegations of his incompetency. While still a captain in the 69th Militia he responded to an offer of a colonel's commission with the admission that "with my limited experience and very imperfect knowledge of military affairs, it would be grievously culpable in me, at this crisis of the National interests, when a great disaster [Bull Run] has to be reversed, to assume a post which I feel, and everybody knows, I am incompetent to fill." Five months later he accepted a commission as a brigadier general.[3]

Meagher was far from alone as a general with minimal military experience in early 1862, however, and none of his men seriously challenged his courage during the time he served as commander of the Irish Brigade. Many of the brigade's officers and enlisted men were soldiers seasoned by wars around the world, and would have given short shrift to any leader who demonstrated overt cowardice or culpable incompetence.

The general does not seem to have studied any military manuals, however, and depended on others to manage the day to day affairs of the brigade and its movements in action. William O'Grady, a former lieutenant in the British Royal Marines who rose from private to captain in the 88th New York, admitted that Meagher was "not excellent as a tactician," but "was worth thousands of men" to the Union for "his magnetism in recruiting." Private Peter Rafferty of the 69th was a bit more caustic, referring to the general as "irrepressible and irresponsible." The casualties suffered by the Irish Brigade resulted not from its commander's incompetence or vague conspiracies, however, but from the brigade's status as an elite unit which would rather fight than run, no matter what the odds, and the poor luck of being in the wrong place at the wrong time.[4]

Meagher's American detractors have, then and now, castigated him for his drinking habits and implied his courage came "in a bottle." Assertions of the general's drunkenness in action surfaced as early as Bull Run, and prominent newspaper correspondent Whitelaw Reid wrote that Meagher "was too drunk to keep the saddle" at Antietam. Several military diarists corroborated Reid's contention. It should be noted, however, that unlike some American born soldiers, Meagher and his Irish Brigade officers made no effort to disguise the fact that they liked their liquor. No doubt some of the stories regarding Meagher's drinking by period diarists and writers had its roots in the anti-immigrant, anti-Catholic feelings shared by many Americans at the time. It should be noted that modern historians are not immune to such prejudices, whether subliminal or otherwise.[5]

It seems quite likely, however, given the historical evidence, that General Meagher drank to excess on a number of occasions. Provost Marshal General Marsena R. Patrick of the Army of the Potomac, a solid Yankee Protestant, characterized Meagher during the general's visit to the

General Meagher in a self designed uniform. (Michael J. McAfee Collection)

army in August of 1864 as "drunk as a Beast & has been so since Monday, sending out his Servant for liquor...." Patrick's version of the Irish American general's behavior on this occasion was sustained by Colonel Theodore B. Gates, post commandant of City Point. Gates noted that Meagher was drunk for a week, until the colonel informed him that he "could not furnish him quarters any longer and he left."[6]

It is also a fact that many Union army officers, who, unlike enlisted men, had generally unrestricted access to commissary whiskey and carried it in their canteens, were often inebriated. Although obvious drunkenness on duty could subject an officer to court martial, it appears that such charges were seldom preferred, and then only when one officer held a grudge against another.

Major General William Henry French, a sometime critic of Meagher, was called "old gin barrel" by his troops, and not only because of his rotund appearance. Marsena Patrick, one of the Army of the Potomac's chief gossip collectors, who was offended by Meagher's drinking habits, also noted that Major General Benjamin Butler had witnessed General Grant drunk on two occasions and was prepared to "use this against him." Colonel William Blaisdell of the 11th Massachusetts, by all accounts a brave and competent officer, was, on at least one occasion, so inebriated that he could not read a map, and one Federal officer counted twenty-nine generals at Spotsylvania so drunk they could barely sit on their horses.[7]

The personable and eloquent Meagher captivated most of the people he encountered, whether Irish or not. William Keeler, a Union navy officer who met the general in 1862, characterized him as "a plain good hearted, well educated Irishman & no doubt...a good officer," as well as "a good talker & an admirable story teller." Keeler, paymaster on the *Monitor*, feared, however, that "like too many others he [Meagher] likes good liquor occasionally. That is the bane of both army & navy and will prove the ruin, I fear, of many a good officer."[8]

Whatever his personal failings, Thomas F. Meagher held a unique place in the hearts of his battle hardened men. When the general bid goodbye to the Irish Brigade in May of 1863, he personally shook the hand of every surviving soldier before leaving the unit. Meagher's subsequent visits to the brigade, most notably on its third birthday, were always occasions of celebration.

General Meagher returned to active duty at the end of 1864, when his resignation was revoked and he was assigned to the western theater. The general arrived in Nashville with no specific assignment in the middle of the presidential campaign of 1864 and almost immediately delivered an oration in support of the Abraham Lincoln/Andrew Johnson ticket, which was widely reprinted and alienated a number of Irish Democrats.

After cooling his heels for awhile, Meagher was assigned to command two ragtag "Provisional Brigades" composed of convalescents, stragglers and replacements assigned to Major General William T. Sherman's army. Since Sherman's force had dispensed with normal lines of communication to slash through the heart of Georgia, there was no ready way for these soldiers to join their units. A far cry from the stalwarts of the Irish Brigade, the men of the Provisional Brigades were assigned to guard the railroad between Chattanooga and Knoxville. In January, 1865, Meagher was ordered to lead what was now called "Meagher's Provisional Division," to join Sherman, who had emerged at Savannah following his successful march to the sea and was driving north through the Carolinas.

General Meagher's command traveled by river steamer to Pittsburgh, thence by rail to Annapolis and then south to New Bern, North Carolina, by ship. The grand progress of the Provisional Division was marked by complaint and dissension. Once again, Meagher himself was accused of inebriation, as were a number of his officers and men. Complaints from staff officers regarding the Irish American general's embarkation schedules at Annapolis almost led to his dismissal by General Grant. By February 13, however, Meagher and his men had all arrived at New Bern. The general was relieved from duty and ordered back to New York a week later. The war was soon over and with it Thomas F. Meagher's career in the United States army. Along with hundreds of other temporary generals, he submitted his resignation on May 12, 1865. It was accepted three days later.

With the conclusion of hostilities, Meagher was rewarded for his wartime service by President Andrew Johnson (for whom he had stumped in the election of 1864) with a position as Secretary of Montana Territory. When the general arrived in the territory in September, 1865, Governor Sidney Edgerton, who had been using his own funds to run Montana, hastily departed for the east and Meagher assumed the responsibilities of administering the territory. Edgerton, a Radical Republican who did not have President Johnson's favor, formally resigned in 1866 and was not immediately replaced, leaving Meagher as de facto governor.

Acting governor Meagher quickly became the focal point of what has been characterized as "one of the most chaotic periods in Montana's political history." Although he was a nominal Democrat before and during the war, Meagher initially sided with Montana's Republicans, probably because many of the territory's Democrats were ex-Rebels or draft dodgers. Many Montana Democrats were Irish, however, providing a ready made base for a politician like Thomas F. Meagher. Perhaps with his eye on a Senate seat with statehood, the general switched sides again, further fueling the territory's political conflagration.[9]

At one point Henry N. Blake, a veteran of the 11th Massachusetts Infantry and editor of the *Montana Post*, so riled Meagher with his editorial policies that the general sent him a letter challenging him to a duel. Blake, a Republican, declined the dangerous honor by mail and "printed both letters in *The Post* under the heading 'Pistols and Coffee for Two.'" Meagher was not one to hold a grudge against a fellow officer, however, and subsequently appointed Blake a militia colonel in an expedition against the Indians.[10]

Montana would, in the end, prove to be the Irish American general's undoing. Meagher arrived at Fort Benton on July 1, 1867, to await a delivery of rifles arriving by Missouri River boat. The general was apprehensive about his enemies and ill with a fever. After a medicinal dose of blackberry wine he went to bed on the docked steamer *G. A. Thompson* with two loaded Colt Navy revolvers by his side.

Sometime that night Meagher mysteriously fell off the *G. A. Thompson*'s deck into the Missouri. The general's body was never recovered and his disappearance has never been satisfactorily explained. Some have speculated that he pitched off the boat following a drinking spree. Perhaps surprisingly, no evidence exists to support this allegation. Others suggest he committed suicide (most unlikely) or even, considering the political temper and culture of Montana Territory, was murdered. While the latter scenario is indeed possible, the answer, as with most things, is very likely the simplest. Meagher, racked with fever, probably awoke, stumbled out on deck, lost his balance and fell overboard.[11]

Whatever happened that night, the world became a less interesting place with Thomas F. Meagher's departure. Down all the years his

Equestrian statue of Brigadier General Thomas Francis Meagher in Helena, Montana. The only known statue of Meagher. (Montana Historical Society)

memory has survived in the ranks of his old regiment, and a tablet commemorates the place of his birth in Waterford. There is, however, no "round tower with a cathedral" to memorialize the man who fathered one of the best infantry brigades that ever was. Instead there is an equestrian statue, thousands of miles from the scene of his greatest fights. Although he strutted but briefly across the sagebrush stage of Montana, Thomas Francis Meagher proudly sits his horse in front of the state capitol in Helena, a manifestation of the pride and patriotism of the Irish of Montana.

Appendix II

The "Wild Geese" -- Irish Exiles in Foreign Service.

It was Hugh O'Neill and Hugh O'Donnell who taught the Irish how to fight someone besides each other, and it was O'Neill who gave them the guns to do the job right. Under his tutelage they bested the armies of Elizabeth I at the Yellow Ford in 1598 and Moyry Pass in 1600. But defeat came to O'Neill, as it would to generations of Irish Rebels, at Kinsale in 1601. Although pardoned, he could no longer live in an Ulster not of his own making and, in 1607, he and Rory O'Donnell and ninety followers left for the continent in what became known as "the flight of the earls."

While many of the earls' men went into European military service and recruited Irishmen for their units, the real beginning of the famed "Wild Geese" dates from 1688, when James II of England, dethroned and at war with his son-in-law and daughter, William and Mary, sent over 5,000 Irish recruits to France in exchange for French regulars. This brigade of expatriates, which became an integral part of the French army, was kept separate from the defeated Irish army brought to France by James' General Patrick Sarsfield after the surrender of Limerick in 1691.

The Treaty of Ryswick in 1698 dissolved James' Irish army in France, but the separate Irish Brigade remained in French service until it was disbanded in 1792 along with the French monarchy. Up to that time, the brigade fought in all of France's wars and, garbed in distinctive red coats, achieved distinction on many fields, chief among them Fontenoy.

Americans owe a debt of gratitude to the French Irish Brigade as well as its Civil War counterpart. During the American War for Independence some soldiers from the brigade's Walsh's Regiment served as marines aboard John Paul Jones' _Bonhomme Richard_. Others, from Dillon's Regiment, fought side by side with American soldiers at Savannah and Yorktown.

The brigade's numerous casualties were replaced by a steady stream of volunteers from Erin. Recruiters slipped into the island and, perhaps aided by the occasional taste of "poteen," enthralled the country lads with the glories of French service. The Irish peasantry, reduced to virtual serfdom under the harsh Penal Laws, were more than willing to take a chance with the French. Since it was illegal for British citizens, which the Irish, however reluctantly, were, to join foreign armies, recruits for the French service were listed as "Wild Geese" on ship manifests. A name heavy with unspoken symbolism, it stuck.

The deeds of the French Irish Brigade became well known to the dispossessed Irish of Connaught through the visits of the recruiting officers and the return of grizzled veterans to the island of their birth. When a small French force landed in the west in 1798, the landless "spalpeens" flocked to the colors – and to brutal deaths in a lost cause.

Irishmen had served Spain since 1585, when the men of Sir Edward Stanley's British regiment, recruited largely in Ireland and serving in the Netherlands, realized they were on the wrong side and defected to the Spanish. While Irish service in the Spanish army was not as continuous as that in the French service, it lasted longer, until the Spanish army's three Irish regiments were disbanded in 1818. The Spanish General Prim recalled this service when he visited General Meagher's Irishmen on the Peninsula in 1862.

It was the achievements of these foreign units, principally the French Irish Brigade, that Thomas F. Meagher had in mind when he formed his own "Irish Brigade" in 1861, rather than the considerable military contributions as individuals and as organized units that Irishmen had made to the British and other armies around the world.

More than mere mercenaries, these seventeenth and eighteenth century Irishmen took the only opportunity afforded them out of grinding poverty and political and religious oppression. As elite troops in foreign lands they garnered more than their share of what passed for glory and what was indeed tragedy. Their spiritual descendants in the Army of the Potomac's Irish Brigade, to this day buried in unknown graves across Maryland, Pennsylvania and Virginia, proved themselves worthy heirs of a distinguished military heritage and, at the same time, claimed for their own posterity the full rights of American citizens. It was shameful that they had to die to do it – but it was ever thus.

Appendix III
Small Arms and the Irish Brigade

The droves of recruits flocking to Federal and Confederate colors at the outbreak of the Civil War clamored for Model 1855 or 1861 .58 caliber muzzle loading rifle muskets, the most modern infantry arms available. Supplies of these guns were, however, limited. Of the 503,000 shoulder arms held in Federal and Northern state arsenals at the outbreak of the war, 400,000 were .69 caliber smoothbores, and 100,000 of the 135,000 small arms either seized or held by Southern states were smoothbores as well. By August of 1861, when Thomas Francis Meager kicked off the Irish Brigade recruiting drive at Jones' Wood, Brigadier General James W. Ripley, Union Chief of Ordnance, had exhausted his reserve supply of rifle muskets.

The men of the 69th New York Volunteers brought a mix of imported Prussian smoothbores and Enfield rifle muskets to Virginia with them, but were reequipped with U. S. Model 1842 .69 caliber smoothbore muskets. The preferred load for these weapons was a .64 or .65 diameter round ball and three buckshot, encased, along with a powder charge, in paper. The soldier would bite off the end of the paper cartridge to expose the powder, ram the cartridge down the muzzle of his musket, then affix a cap on the nipple or "cone" underneath the hammer. When the trigger released the cocked hammer it hit the explosive cap and ignited the charge in the gun.

Although his Company K Zouaves carried **rifled** .69 caliber muskets, conversions of older smoothbores using the hollow based "minie ball," General Meagher preferred smoothbores for all his regiments because he thought much of the Irish Brigade's fighting "would be at very close quarters." William O'Grady of the 88th New York recalled afterward, however, that "sometimes our short range weapons were a disadvantage." O'Grady was one of the men who "found" rifle muskets to silence Confederate skirmishers on the brigade front at Antietam.[1]

Many army officers, assuming that most fights would take place at seventy-five yards or less, agreed with Meagher's small arms choice. As late as 1863, Colonel George L. Willard of the 125th New York flatly stated that, for most military purposes, the smoothbore musket was actually better than its rifled relative. Although he conceded the rifle musket's accuracy over longer ranges, Willard asserted that the necessity to change sight settings during the course of combat, especially when infantrymen faced a fast closing cavalry charge, was too confusing for average troops. He believed infantrymen would do better to hold their fire until the horsemen were close and then deliver a withering volley of buck and ball. According to Willard, "decisive victories cannot be gained by firing at long ranges; at short ranges the buck and ball cartridge is certainly more effective."[2]

In fact, throughout the Civil War, cavalrymen were generally very reluctant to charge infantry armed with anything, but Meagher and Willard's general philosophy might not have been too far off the mark, at least in the war's early years. British military historian Paddy Griffith has asserted that the types of small arms used by opponents in Civil War battles mattered little because the tactics (or lack of same) employed by officers on both sides led to essentially short-range firefights in which the accuracy of the individual or his weapon was largely irrelevant. If this is true, then the .69 caliber smoothbore may have had an advantage over the rifle musket in most fights, as a buck and ball load gave the shooter four chances to kill or disable his enemy. Most authorities thought buck and ball effective up to 100 yards, which Griffith states was the average distance of a firefight during the first two years of the war.

In a test conducted in Texas in 1855, soldiers firing .69 caliber buck and ball rounds at a six foot by eighteen inch target 100 yards away scored as many hits with their Model 1842 smoothbore muskets as a company armed with .54 caliber Model 1841 rifles firing patched round balls when each group fired a specified number of rounds. Although buckshot's lethality at that distance can be fairly questioned, a wound does not have to be fatal or even serious to be tactically effective. In most cases, a wounded man will quickly leave the immediate scene of battle and may require one or more other men to help him off. Due to a lack of surgical antisepsis, minor wounds during the Civil War often proved fatal or disabling far out of proportion to their initial damage.

By mid 1862, many soldiers who had clamored for rifle muskets had modified their previously dim view of smoothbores. Colonel Robert McAllister, commander of the 11th New Jersey, was not unhappy when eight of his ten companies traded in their Austrian rifles for smoothbore muskets. McAllister wrote that "it is now thought that the musket with buck and ball is after all the best arm in the service." The 12th Rhode Island and 12th New Hampshire, raised like the 11th in 1862, received the same mix of imported rifles and native smoothbores.[3]

The companies armed with rifles in these regiments were the "flank" companies. Longer range guns were considered desirable for men who could protect a regiment or brigade's vulnerable flanks by delivering accurate long range fire on an attacking force. The flank companies were also used as skirmishers, for whom individual marksmanship against specific targets was highly valued. Marksmanship was stressed, at least theoretically, for soldiers serving in flank companies.

The 28th Massachusetts, which joined the Irish Brigade just before Fredericksburg, was armed with Enfield rifle muskets. The Bay State men retained their Enfields and were often detailed as brigade skirmishers or flankers. So much so, in fact, that a Massachusetts officer complained of the "arduous" duty. The remainder of the brigade's regiments, the 63rd, 69th and 88th New York and the 116th Pennsylvania, retained smoothbore muskets far beyond the end of the Meagher era. These Irish Brigade outfits were among the twenty-six, or 10.5% of Federal regiments in the Army of the Potomac still armed in whole or in part with smoothbore muskets at the battle of Gettysburg.

When infusions of large numbers of recruits led to the formation of new companies for the New York and Pennsylvania regiments over the winter of 1863-1864, the new men were issued smoothbores, at a time when rifle muskets were again in good supply. The only rationale for such a peculiarity would be that the tactical doctrine symbolized by the smoothbore musket was still ascendant in the brigade. The rest of the army, however, was beginning to realize the potential of the rifle musket, and, for the first time in the Army of the Potomac, an organized program of target practice was established in the spring of 1864.

With the notable exception of the 28th Massachusetts, smoothbores remained standard issue in the Irish Brigade until the brigade was temporarily broken up in June of 1864. Although sorry to leave their Irish comrades, the Pennsylvanians of the 116th were delighted to finally turn in their smoothbores for rifle muskets. In the course of Grant's overland campaign, fighting distances had stretched out so that opponents were often firing at each other at ranges up to 200 yards, which was, by the standards of the day, "long range."

Surviving ordnance reports indicate that the brigade's New York regiments exchanged their smoothbores for rifle muskets at around the same time the Pennsylvanians did. The switch probably coincided with the creation of the "Consolidated Brigade." Unlike the men of the 116th, the New Yorkers left no record of whether or not they approved the change. There were, however, no complaints registered either.

The following Ordnance reports for the Irish Brigade's core regiments, the 28th, 63rd, 69th, 88th and 116th, were abstracted from the Union army's compiled ordnance reports on file in the National Archives by William C. Goble. Each company commander in the army was responsible for turning in a quarterly ordnance return to his regimental commander, who, in turn, turned in a regimental return.

The existing records are incomplete, for various reasons. Records were often not turned in in the immediate wake of disastrous battles. For example, only one company of the 69th New York, a regiment which lost *all* of its officers killed or wounded at Fredericksburg, handed in an ordnance return for the Fourth Quarter of 1862.

Other records may well not be accurate because the officer or clerk filling the form out checked the wrong column. The 69th New York is listed as having Model 1842 smoothbores in one quarter, then older model flintlock smoothbores converted to percussion in the next quarter, then Model 1842s the following quarter. It is more likely that the wrong column was checked rather than that the regiment was issued different weapons in successive quarters. Other quarters were simply not turned in by deceased or careless officers, or were lost somewhere between the field and the War Department in the 130 years that have intervened. For similar reasons, the reports of individual companies are often missing. It should be remembered, however, that the 116th and the three New York regiments were consolidated in 1863, then expanded again in 1864. The 28th Massachusetts was consolidated following the discharge of veterans who had not reenlisted in late 1864.

A careful perusal suggests that certain peculiarities existed at times in different regiments. The 28th Massachusetts, for example, reports a sole "US Rifle with Sword Bayonet," (a modified Model 1841 or a Model 1855) in most companies for the first quarter of 1863. Company A con-

150

tinues to report one of these arms throughout the year. Similarly, Springfield .58 caliber rifle muskets show up here and there and are, no doubt, battlefield pickups to replace damaged arms or to supply more adequate rifled weapons for skirmishing duties.

With all their inherent defects, however, the records buttress the testimony of the brigade's soldiers that, for a longer period in time than in any other outfit in the Army of the Potomac, save perhaps the 12th New Jersey Infantry, the majority of the men of the Irish Brigade carried smoothbore muskets into battle.

TWENTY EIGHTH MASSACHUSETTS
QUARTERLY ORDNANCE REPORTS

FOURTH QUARTER 1862
CO. A	ENFIELD RIFLE-MUSKET	90
CO. B	ENFIELD RIFLE-MUSKET	90
CO. C	ENFIELD RIFLE-MUSKET	90
CO. D	ENFIELD RIFLE-MUSKET	90
CO. E	ENFIELD RIFLE-MUSKET	90
CO. F	ENFIELD RIFLE-MUSKET	89
CO. G	ENFIELD RIFLE-MUSKET	90
CO. H	ENFIELD RIFLE-MUSKET	88
CO. I		NR
CO. K	ENFIELD RIFLE-MUSKET	89

FIRST QUARTER 1863
CO. A	ENFIELD RIFLE-MUSKET	35
	SPRINGFIELD RIFLE-MUSKET	1
	US RIFLE W/ SWORD BAYONET	1
CO. B		NR
CO. C	ENFIELD RIFLE-MUSKET	34
	US RIFLE W/ SWORD BAYONET	1
CO. D	ENFIELD RIFLE-MUSKET	35
CO. E	ENFIELD RIFLE-MUSKET	26
	SPRINGFIELD RIFLE-MUSKET	3
	US RIFLE W/ SWORD BAYONET	1
CO. F	ENFIELD RIFLE-MUSKET	23
	US RIFLE W/ SWORD BAYONET	1
CO. G	ENFIELD RIFLE-MUSKET	31
CO. H	ENFIELD RIFLE-MUSKET	25
	US RIFLE W/ SWORD BAYONET	1
CO. I	ENFIELD RIFLE-MUSKET	28
	US RIFLE W/ SWORD BAYONET	1
CO. K	ENFIELD RIFLE-MUSKET	29
	SPRINGFIELD RIFLE-MUSKET	1
	US RIFLE W/ SWORD BAYONET	1

SECOND QUARTER 1863
CO. A	ENFIELD RIFLE-MUSKET	NR
CO. B	ENFIELD RIFLE-MUSKET	28
CO. C	ENFIELD RIFLE-MUSKET	30
	US RIFLE W/ SWORD BAYONET	1

```
CO. D    ENFIELD RIFLE-MUSKET .................................................. 32
CO. E             .......................................................................... NR
CO. F    ENFIELD RIFLE-MUSKET .................................................. 18
         US RIFLE W/ SWORD BAYONET .......................................  1
CO. G    ENFIELD RIFLE-MUSKET .................................................. 29
CO. H    ENFIELD RIFLE-MUSKET .................................................. 20
CO. I    ENFIELD RIFLE-MUSKET .................................................. 31
         US RIFLE W/ SWORD BAYONET .......................................  1
CO. K    ENFIELD RIFLE-MUSKET .................................................. 27
         SPRINGFIELD RIFLE-MUSKET ..........................................  1
         US RIFLE W/SWORD BAYONET .........................................  1
```

THIRD QUARTER 1863

```
CO. A    ENFIELD RIFLE-MUSKET .................................................. 28
         US RIFLE W/ SWORD BAYONET .......................................  1
CO. B    ENFIELD RIFLE-MUSKET .................................................. 28
CO. C    ENFIELD RIFLE-MUSKET .................................................. 39
CO. D             .......................................................................... NR
CO. E    ENFIELD RIFLE-MUSKET .................................................. 26
CO. F    ENFIELD RIFLE-MUSKET .................................................. 26
CO. G    ENFIELD RIFLE-MUSKET .................................................. 29
CO. H    ENFIELD RIFLE-MUSKET .................................................. 19
CO. I    ENFIELD RIFLE-MUSKET .................................................. 31
CO. K             .......................................................................... NR
```

FOURTH QUARTER 1863

```
CO. A    ENFIELD RIFLE-MUSKET .................................................. 25
         US RIFLE W/ SWORD BAYONET .......................................  1
CO. B    ENFIELD RIFLE-MUSKET .................................................. 27
CO. C             .......................................................................... NR
CO. D    ENFIELD RIFLE-MUSKET .................................................. 14
CO. E    ENFIELD RIFLE-MUSKET .................................................. 28
CO. F    ENFIELD RIFLE-MUSKET .................................................. 25
CO. G    ENFIELD RIFLE-MUSKET .................................................. 20
CO. H    ENFIELD RIFLE-MUSKET .................................................. 18
CO. I    ENFIELD RIFLE-MUSKET .................................................. 35
CO. K             .......................................................................... NR
```

FIRST QUARTER 1864

```
CO. A    ENFIELD RIFLE-MUSKET .................................................. 44
CO. B             .......................................................................... NR
CO. C    ENFIELD RIFLE-MUSKET .................................................. 41
CO. D    ENFIELD RIFLE-MUSKET .................................................. 32
```

CO. E	ENFIELD RIFLE-MUSKET	44
CO. F	ENFIELD RIFLE-MUSKET	43
CO. G	ENFIELD RIFLE-MUSKET	40
CO. H	ENFIELD RIFLE-MUSKET	32
CO. I		NR
CO. K		NR

SECOND QUARTER 1864

CO. A	ENFIELD RIFLE-MUSKET	11
CO. B		NR
CO. C	ENFIELD RIFLE-MUSKET	15
CO. D	ENFIELD RIFLE-MUSKET	10
CO. E		NR
CO. F	ENFIELD RIFLE-MUSKET	6
CO. G	ENFIELD RIFLE-MUSKET	13
CO. H	ENFIELD RIFLE-MUSKET	14
CO. I		NR
CO. K	ENFIELD RIFLE-MUSKET	10

THIRD QUARTER 1864

CO. A	ENFIELD RIFLE-MUSKET	17
CO. B	ENFIELD RIFLE-MUSKET	14
CO. C	ENFIELD RIFLE-MUSKET	18
CO. D	ENFIELD RIFLE-MUSKET	10
CO. E	ENFIELD RIFLE-MUSKET	19
CO. F	ENFIELD RIFLE-MUSKET	17
CO. G	ENFIELD RIFLE-MUSKET	4
CO. H	ENFIELD RIFLE-MUSKET	120
CO. I	ENFIELD RIFLE-MUSKET	10
CO. K	ENFIELD RIFLE-MUSKET	14

FOURTH QUARTER 1864

CO. A	ENFIELD RIFLE-MUSKET	35
CO. B	ENFIELD RIFLE-MUSKET	29
CO. C	RIFLE-MUSKET	30
CO. D		NR
CO. E	ENFIELD RIFLE-MUSKET	31
CO. F	ENFIELD RIFLE-MUSKET	10
CO. G		NR
CO. H	ENFIELD RIFLE-MUSKET	7
CO. I	SPRINGFIELD RIFLE-MUSKET	20
CO. K		NR

SIXTY-THIRD NEW YORK
QUARTERLY ORDNANCE REPORTS

FOURTH QUARTER 1862
CO. A	MODEL 1842 MUSKET	18
	SPRINGFIELD RIFLE-MUSKET	1
CO. B	MODEL 1842 MUSKET	10
	SPRINGFIELD RIFLE-MUSKET	1
CO. C	MODEL 1842 MUSKET	12
CO. D	MODEL 1842 MUSKET	12
CO. E	MODEL 1842 MUSKET	14
CO. F	MODEL 1842 MUSKET	13
	SPRINGFIELD RIFLE-MUSKET	1
CO. G	MODEL 1842 MUSKET	18
	SPRINGFIELD RIFLE-MUSKET	3
CO. H	MODEL 1842 MUSKET	13
CO. I	MODEL 1842 MUSKET	1
CO. K	MODEL 1842 MUSKET	14

FIRST QUARTER 1863
CO. A	SMOOTHBORE MUSKET ALTERED TO PERCUSSION	20
CO. B	SMOOTHBORE MUSKET ALTERED TO PERCUSSION	10
CO. C	SMOOTHBORE MUSKET ALTERED TO PERCUSSION	10
CO. D	SMOOTHBORE MUSKET ALTERED TO PERCUSSION	17
CO. E	SMOOTHBORE MUSKET ALTERED TO PERCUSSION	32
CO. F	SMOOTHBORE MUSKET ALTERED TO PERCUSSION	11
CO. G	SMOOTHBORE MUSKET ALTERED TO PERCUSSION	24
CO. H	SMOOTHBORE MUSKET ALTERED TO PERCUSSION	11
CO. I	SMOOTHBORE MUSKET ALTERED TO PERCUSSION	7
CO. K	SMOOTHBORE MUSKET ALTERED TO PERCUSSION	18
RQM	SMOOTHBORE MUSKET ALTERED TO PERCUSSION	4

SECOND QUARTER 1863
CO. A		NR
CO. B	MODEL 1842 MUSKET	39
	ENFIELD RIFLE-MUSKET	1
CO. C		NR
CO. D		NR
CO. E		NR
CO. F		NR
CO. G		NR
CO. H		NR

CO. I .... NR
CO. K .... N

THIRD QUARTER 1863
CO. A   RIFLED MUSKET ALTERED TO PERCUSSION 44
CO. B   RIFLED MUSKET ALTERED TO PERCUSSION 42
         ENFIELD RIFLE-MUSKET 1
CO. C .... NR
CO. D .... NR
CO. E .... NR
CO. F .... NR
CO. G .... NR
CO. H .... NR
CO. I .... NR
CO. K .... NR

FOURTH QUARTER 1863
CO. A .... NR
CO. B   MODEL 1842 MUSKET 26
         SPRINGFIELD RIFLE-MUSKET 4
CO. C .... NR
CO. D .... NR
CO. E   ENFIELD RIFLE-MUSKET 40
         MODEL 1842 MUSKET 24
         SPRINGFIELD RIFLE-MUSKET 1
CO. F .... NR
CO. G .... NR
CO. H   MODEL 1842 MUSKET 27
CO. I .... NR
CO. K .... NR

FIRST QUARTER 1864
CO. A   MODEL 1842 MUSKET 30
CO. B   MODEL 1842 MUSKET 34
         SPRINGFIELD RIFLE-MUSKET 4
CO. C .... NR
CO. D .... NR
CO. E .... NR
CO. F .... NR
CO. G .... NR
CO. H .... NR
CO. I .... NR
CO. K .... NR

SECOND QUARTER 1864

CO. A		NR
CO. B		NR
CO. C	ENFIELD RIFLE-MUSKET	9
	SPRINGFIELD RIFLE-MUSKET	3
CO. D	MODEL 1842 MUSKET	12
CO. E		NR
CO. F		NR
CO. G		NR
CO. H		NR
CO. I		NR
CO. K		NR

THIRD QUARTER 1864

CO. A	SPRINGFIELD RIFLE-MUSKET	8
	ENFIELD RIFLE-MUSKET	3
CO. B		NR
CO. C	ENFIELD RIFLE-MUSKET	11
	SPRINGFIELD RIFLE-MUSKET	3
CO. D	SPRINGFIELD RIFLE-MUSKET	6
CO. E	SPRINGFIELD RIFLE-MUSKET	11
	ENFIELD RIFLE-MUSKET	6
CO. F	SPRINGFIELD RIFLE-MUSKET	17
	ENFIELD RIFLE-MUSKET	5
CO. G		NR
CO. H		NR
CO. I		NR
CO. K		NR

FOURTH QUARTER 1864

CO. A	SPRINGFIELD RIFLE-MUSKET	14
	ENFIELD RIFLE-MUSKET	2
CO. B	ENFIELD RIFLE-MUSKET	6
	SPRINGFIELD RIFLE-MUSKET	5
CO. C	ENFIELD RIFLE-MUSKET	10
	SPRINGFIELD RIFLE-MUSKET	7
CO. D	SPRINGFIELD RIFLE-MUSKET	3
CO. E	SPRINGFIELD RIFLE-MUSKET	15
	ENFIELD RIFLE-MUSKET	3
CO. F	SPRINGFIELD RIFLE-MUSKET	26
	ENFIELD RIFLE-MUSKET	5
CO. G		NR
CO. H		NR

| CO. I | .... NR |
| CO. K | .... NR |

SIXTY-NINTH NEW YORK
QUARTERLY ORDNANCE REPORTS

FOURTH QUARTER 1862
CO. A	.... NR
CO. B	.... NR
CO. C	MODEL 1842 MUSKET 14
CO. D	.... NR
CO. E	.... NR
CO. F	.... NR
CO. G	.... NR
CO. H	.... NR
CO. I	.... NR
CO. K	.... NR

FIRST QUARTER 1863
CO. A	SMOOTHBORE MUSKET ALTERED TO PERCUSSION 23
CO. B	SMOOTHBORE MUSKET ALTERED TO PERCUSSION 16
CO. C	SMOOTHBORE MUSKET ALTERED TO PERCUSSION 17
CO. D	SMOOTHBORE MUSKET ALTERED TO PERCUSSION 15
CO. E	SMOOTHBORE MUSKET ALTERED TO PERCUSSION 17
CO. F	SMOOTHBORE MUSKET ALTERED TO PERCUSSION 7
CO. G	SMOOTHBORE MUSKET ALTERED TO PERCUSSION 14
CO. H	SMOOTHBORE MUSKET ALTERED TO PERCUSSION 7
CO. I	SMOOTHBORE MUSKET ALTERED TO PERCUSSION 21
CO. K	SMOOTHBORE MUSKET ALTERED TO PERCUSSION 17

SECOND QUARTER 1863
CO. A	MODEL 1842 MUSKET 51
CO. B	MODEL 1842 MUSKET 49
CO. C	.... NR
CO. D	.... NR
CO. E	.... NR
CO. F	.... NR
CO. G	.... NR
CO. H	.... NR
CO. I	.... NR
CO. K	.... NR

159

EIGHTY-EIGHTH NEW YORK
QUARTERLY ORDNANCE REPORTS

CO. I .... NR
CO. K .... NR

FIRST QUARTER 1863
CO. A   SMOOTHBORE MUSKET ALTERED TO PERCUSSION.................. 18
CO. B   SMOOTHBORE MUSKET ALTERED TO PERCUSSION.................. 12
CO. C   SMOOTHBORE MUSKET ALTERED TO PERCUSSION.................. 16
CO. D .... NR
CO. E   SMOOTHBORE MUSKET ALTERED TO PERCUSSION.................. 16
CO. F   SMOOTHBORE MUSKET ALTERED TO PERCUSSION.................. 12
CO. G   SMOOTHBORE MUSKET ALTERED TO PERCUSSION.................. 21
CO. H   SMOOTHBORE MUSKET ALTERED TO PERCUSSION.................. 16
CO. I   SMOOTHBORE MUSKET ALTERED TO PERCUSSION.................. 23
CO. K   SMOOTHBORE MUSKET ALTERED TO PERCUSSION.................. 27

SECOND QUARTER 1863
CO. A .... NR
CO. B .... NR
CO. C   MODEL 1842 MUSKET 13
CO. D .... NR
CO. E .... NR
CO. F .... NR
CO. G .... NR
CO. H .... NR
CO. I   MODEL 1842 MUSKET 14
CO. K .... NR

THIRD QUARTER 1863
CO. A   AUSTRIAN RIFLE-MUSKET 34
          MODEL 1842 MUSKET 30
CO. B .... NR
CO. C .... NR
CO. D .... NR
CO. E .... NR
CO. F .... NR
CO. G .... NR
CO. H .... NR
CO. I .... NR
CO. K .... NR

FOURTH QUARTER 1863
CO. A   MODEL 1842 MUSKET 29
CO. B .... NR

```
CO. C    ..................................................................................  NR
CO. D    ..................................................................................  NR
CO. E    ..................................................................................  NR
CO. F    ..................................................................................  NR
CO. G    ..................................................................................  NR
CO. H    ..................................................................................  NR
CO. I    ..................................................................................  NR
CO. K    ..................................................................................  NR
```

FIRST QUARTER 1864
```
CO. A    MODEL 1842 MUSKET ..................................................  3
CO. B    ..................................................................................  NR
CO. C    ..................................................................................  NR
CO. D    ..................................................................................  NR
CO. E    ..................................................................................  NR
CO. F    ..................................................................................  NR
CO. G    ..................................................................................  NR
CO. H    ..................................................................................  NR
CO. I    ..................................................................................  NR
CO. K    ..................................................................................  NR
RQM      MODEL 1842 MUSKET ..............................................  216
```

SECOND QUARTER 1864
```
CO. A    MODEL 1842 MUSKET ..............................................  17
         SPRINGFIELD RIFLE-MUSKET ...................................  6
         ENFIELD RIFLE-MUSKET ...........................................  6
CO. B    MODEL 1842 MUSKET ..............................................  19
         SPRINGFIELD RIFLE-MUSKET ...................................  5
         ENFIELD RIFLE-MUSKET ...........................................  3
CO. C    MODEL 1842 MUSKET ..............................................  28
CO. D    ..................................................................................  NR
CO. E    ..................................................................................  NR
CO. F    ..................................................................................  NR
CO. G    ..................................................................................  NR
CO. H    ..................................................................................  NR
CO. I    ..................................................................................  NR
CO. K    ..................................................................................  NR
RQM      MODEL 1842 MUSKET ..............................................  216
```

THIRD QUARTER 1864
```
CO. A    SPRINGFIELD RIFLE-MUSKET ...................................  26
CO. B    SPRINGFIELD RIFLE-MUSKET ...................................  18
         ENFIELD RIFLE-MUSKET ...........................................  2
```

CO. C	SPRINGFIELD RIFLE-MUSKET	9
CO. D	SPRINGFIELD RIFLE-MUSKET	21
CO. E	SPRINGFIELD RIFLE-MUSKET	14
	ENFIELD RIFLE-MUSKET	3
CO. F		NR
CO. H		NR
CO. I		NR
CO. K		NR

FOURTH QUARTER 1864

CO. A		NR
CO. B	SPRINGFIELD RIFLE-MUSKET	24
	ENFIELD RIFLE-MUSKET	2
CO. C	SPRINGFIELD RIFLE-MUSKET	8
	ENFIELD RIFLE-MUSKET	9
CO. D	SPRINGFIELD RIFLE-MUSKET	18
CO. E	SPRINGFIELD RIFLE-MUSKET	14
	ENFIELD RIFLE-MUSKET	3
CO. F		NR
CO. G		NR
CO. H		NR
CO. I		NR
CO. K		NR

ONE HUNDRED AND SIXTEENTH PENNSYLVANIA
QUARTERLY ORDNANCE REPORTS

FOURTH QUARTER 1862

CO. A		NR
CO. B		NR
CO. C	ENFIELD RIFLE-MUSKET	24
CO. D		NR
CO. E	MODEL 1842 MUSKET	11
CO. F		NR
CO. G	MODEL 1842 MUSKET	16
CO. H	MODEL 1842 MUSKET	17
CO. I	MODEL 1842 MUSKET	31
CO. K		NR

FIRST QUARTER 1863

CO. A	MODEL 1842 MUSKET	44
CO. B	MODEL 1842 MUSKET	52
CO. C		NR
CO. D	MODEL 1842 MUSKET	39
CO. E		NR
CO. F		NR
CO. G		NR
CO. H		NR
CO. I		NR
CO. K		NR

SECOND QUARTER 1863

CO. A	MODEL 1842 MUSKET	30
CO. B	MODEL 1842 MUSKET	45
CO. C		NR
CO. D	MODEL 1842 MUSKET	36
CO. E		NR
CO. F		NR
CO. G		NR
CO. H		NR
CO. I		NR
CO. K		NR

THIRD QUARTER 1863

CO. A	MODEL 1842 MUSKET	19
CO. B	MODEL 1842 MUSKET	42
CO. C	MODEL 1842 MUSKET	31
CO. D	MODEL 1842 MUSKET	22
CO. E		NR
CO. F		NR
CO. G		NR
CO. H		NR
CO. I		NR
CO. K		NR

FOURTH QUARTER 1863

CO. A	MODEL 1842 MUSKET	23
CO. B	MODEL 1842 MUSKET	40
CO. C	MODEL 1842 MUSKET	30
CO. D	MODEL 1842 MUSKET	22
CO. E		NR
CO. F		NR

CO. G		NR
CO. H		NR
CO. I		NR
CO. K		NR

FIRST QUARTER 1864

CO. A		NR
CO. B	MODEL 1842 MUSKET	42
CO. C	MODEL 1842 MUSKET	40
CO. D	MODEL 1842 MUSKET	26
CO. E		NR
CO. F	MODEL 1842 MUSKET	115
CO. G	MODEL 1842 MUSKET	22
CO. H	MODEL 1842 MUSKET	91
CO. I		NR
CO. K		NR
RQM	MODEL 1842 MUSKET	20

SECOND QUARTER 1864

CO. A	MODEL 1842 MUSKET	29
CO. B		NR
CO. C	MODEL 1842 MUSKET	27
CO. D	MODEL 1842 MUSKET	34
CO. E	MODEL 1842 MUSKET	12
CO. F	MODEL 1842 MUSKET	28
CO. G	MODEL 1842 MUSKET	35
CO. H	MODEL 1842 MUSKET	7
CO. I	MODEL 1842 MUSKET	5
CO. K		NR
RQM	MODEL 1842 MUSKET	7

THIRD QUARTER 1864

CO. A	SPRINGFIELD RIFLE-MUSKET	3
CO. B		NR
CO. C	SPRINGFIELD RIFLE-MUSKET	14
CO. D	SPRINGFIELD RIFLE-MUSKET	22
	ENFIELD RIFLE-MUSKET	2
CO. E	SPRINGFIELD RIFLE-MUSKET	24
CO. F	SPRINGFIELD RIFLE-MUSKET	27
CO. G	SPRINGFIELD RIFLE-MUSKET	21
CO. H	SPRINGFIELD RIFLE-MUSKET	15
CO. I	SPRINGFIELD RIFLE-MUSKET	29
CO. K	SPRINGFIELD RIFLE-MUSKET	13

Photo Gallery

A member of the Phoenix Zouaves, a pre-war Irish American military unit in New York City with which Thomas Francis Meagher was associated. (Michael J. McAfee Collection)

Officers of the 69th New York State Militia in their original green uniform in the mid-1850s. (Lt. Col. Kenneth H. Powers Collection.)

Private, 69th Militia, 1861, dress uniform. (Michael J. McAfee Collection)

Private, 69th Militia, 1861, fatigue uniform. (Michael J. McAfee Collection)

Postwar picture of Levi Curtis Brackett. The Irish born Brackett served as sergeant major and first lieutenant in the 28th Massachusetts before being appointed Captain of Company B, 57th Massachusetts. Brackett was breveted major while serving as a IX Corps staff officer in 1864. He was wounded in front of Marye's Heights at Fredericksburg while serving with the 28th. (USAMHI)

Lieutenant Colonel George W. Cartwright, 28th Massachusetts, with First Division, II Corps insignia on his hat. Dublin born, Cartwright served in the 12th New York Militia in 1861 and then the 12th New York Volunteers before transferring to the 28th as adjutant. Promoted to major, Cartwright commanded the 28th at James Island in June of 1862 and then was badly wounded at Second Bull Run. He served with the 28th until discharged on December 20, 1864. George's father, Thomas W. Cartwright, served as a captain in the 63rd New York. (USAMHI)

Samuel Chapman, Companies E and I, 28th Massachusetts. Chapman joined the 28th on August 25, 1862, reenlisted January 1, 1864 and was discharged July 21, 1865. He was wounded May 5, 1864 in the Wilderness. (Joe Maghe Collection)

First Lieutenant Addison A. Hosner, 28th Massachusetts. (USAMHI)

Private Patrick Kelly, Company B, 28th Massachusetts. (Charles B. Oellig Collection)

Captain James Magner, Company I, 28th Massachusetts. A resident of Minnesota and an experienced Indian fighter, Magner resigned a position on the staff of General David Hunter in order to serve as a line officer in the 28th. A gregarious and popular officer, he was killed in action at Spotsylvania on May 18, 1864. (USAMHI)

Private William McFarlane, 28th Massachusetts, in his postwar GAR uniform. (MASS/MOLLUS/USAMHI)

Lieutenant Colonel James D. Brady, 63rd New York, in a postwar photo.
Brady joined the 63rd in early 1862 as adjutant. He served in staff positions
in the Irish Brigade, First Division and II Corps and was the last commander
of the 63rd. (MOL-PA/USAMHI)

Second Lieutenant Jerome Connelly, Company D, 63rd New York. (Michael J. McAfee Collection)

Colonel Michael Corcoran, 69th New York Militia, 1861. (Michael J. McAfee Collection)

Captain John Dwyer, 63rd New York. Dwyer fought as a lieutenant at
Fredericksburg, where he remembered an order to "lie down and fire.
Fortunately...or not a man or officer would have lived."
(NYSAG/USAMHI)

First Lieutenant James E. Mackey, 63rd New York. Born in Buffalo, New York, Mackey served on General Meagher's staff and was mortally wounded September 17, 1862 at Antietam. He died at home the following month. (NYSAG/USAMHI)

First Lieutenant James McQuade, 63rd New York. (Michael J. McAfee Collection)

Captain Michael O'Sullivan, 63rd New York. The Dublin born O'Sullivan recruited the 63rd's Company E, which he commanded until wounded in the knee at Antietam. He was mustered out due to the wound. (NYSAG/ USAMHI)

Second Lieutenant David P. Rood, Company E, 63rd New York. (Lt. Col. Kenneth H. Powers Collection)

First Lieutenant Charles Lewis, (l.) 36th New York and Second Lieutenant
James Scott, 63rd New York. (NYSAG/USAMHI)

Major Thomas Touhy, 63rd New York. Born in County Clare, Touhy joined the 63rd as a second lieutenant in August, 1861. Described as a "gallant, unassuming officer," Touhy served with his regiment through May 5, 1864, when he was mortally wounded in the Wilderness. (NYSAG/USAMHI)

Lawrence Cahill, 69th New York. A veteran of the 69th Militia, where he served as an ordnance sergeant and second lieutenant of Company B, Cahill joined the 69th Volunteers as a first lieutenant of that outfit's Company B. He was badly wounded in the right leg at Malvern Hill and served subsequently in the Veteran Reserve Corps. (Joe Maghe Collection)

James Cavanaugh, the "little major" of the 69th New York Volunteers, was a Tipperary man. Badly wounded at Fredericksburg, Cavanaugh was discharged, but later served with the 69th Militia. (USAMHI)

Lieutenant Charles Clark, 69th and 88th New York. (Michael J. McAfee Collection)

Colonel Michael Corcoran of the 69th Militia. (MASS/MOLLUS/USAMHI)

Private Patrick Henry Coyle, 69th New York, in civilian clothes. (USAMHI)

Captain John H. Donovan, 69th New York. This picture was taken after Malvern Hill, where Donovan was shot through the eye. Wounded again at Fredericksburg, he was transferred to the Veteran Reserve Corps for the rest of the war. (Martin L. Schoenfeld Collection)

Major Thomas Lynch, 63rd New York. Major Lynch died at Camp California in December, 1861. (Lt. Col. Kenneth H. Powers Collection)

Thomas Francis Meagher had an extensive uniform wardrobe. He probably designed this outfit for field use. (Michael J. McAfee Collection)

Captain Garret Nagle, 69th New York. Nagle, a collateral descendent of the famed Edmund Burke, was badly wounded in the right shoulder at Antietam and finished his war in the Veteran Reserve Corps. His hat insignia features a wreath of shamrocks topped by a "69." The "1" in the center of the wreath indicates that the 69th was the "First Regiment Irish Brigade." (Jack McCormack collection)

Colonel Robert Nugent, 69th New York Volunteers. (Michael J. MacAfee Collection)

Private John M. Reynolds, 69th New York. (Bud Scully Collection)

Captain Dennis L. Sullivan, 69th New York. Born in Halifax, Nova Scotia of Irish parents, Sullivan served as regimental quartermaster. He helped rally the 20th New York when that regiment was driven back at White Oak Swamp on the Peninsula. (NYSAG/USAMHI)

Private George F. Wright, 69th New York. (NYSAG/USAMHI)

Dublin born Colonel Henry Baker, 88th New York, in a postwar picture. Baker's wife and sister, who were with him in camp, helped host the party celebrating General Meagher's assumption of the command of the Irish Brigade in February, 1862. (USAMHI)

John J. Blake, 69th and 88th New York. Commissioned a second lieutenant in the 88th's Company B in 1861, Blake rose to the rank of captain before being mustered out when the regiment was consolidated into a two company battalion in 1863. He returned to duty as a second lieutenant in the 69th's Company K in January, 1864, and was again promoted to captain. Blake was wounded and captured at Spotsylvania on May 12, 1864. He died of his wound in Richmond on June 3, 1864. (Michael J. McAfee Collection)

Captain Patrick Ryder, Company B, 88th New York. Ryder was killed in action in the Wilderness. (NYSAG/USAMHI)

Private William Tighe, 88th New York. (NYSAG/USAMHI)

Private John H. Hoffman, 116th Pennsylvania. (USAMHI)

First Sergeant Edward S. Kline, Company F, 116th Pennsylvania. Kline was wounded at Reams' Station, August 25, 1864. This picture was probably taken at the end of the war, as Sergeant Kline is wearing his veteran chevron on his sleeve. (MOL-PA/USAMHI)

Private David McCullough, Company D, 116th Pennsylvania, 1862-1865. McCullough appears to be carrying a Model 1842 .69 caliber smoothbore musket. (USAMHI)

Captain Garrett St. Patrick Nowlen, Company D, 116th Pennsylvania, was born in Philadelphia of Irish parents. Former adjutant of the regiment, Nowlen commanded the 116th at Reams Station, August 25, 1864, where he was killed in action. He was buried at Laurel Hill Cemetery in Philadelphia. (USAMHI)

Captain John O'Neill, Company K, 116th Pennsylvania. After fighting Rebels in Missouri in 1861, O'Neill traveled east, where he joined the 116th. The captain was badly wounded in the 116th's first fight at Fredericksburg, and was transferred to the Veteran Reserve Corps on April 4, 1863. (USAMHI)

Colonel Corcoran and staff of the 69th New York Militia. The officer second from the right may be Captain (acting lieutenant colonel) James Haggerty. (Michael J. McAfee Collection)

Captain Thomas Francis Meagher and members of his Company K "Irish Zouaves" of the 69th Militia in Virginia, 1861. (Michael J. McAfee Collection)

Officers of the 69th New York Militia and friends outside Washington, probably at Fort Corcoran, 1861. Colonel Corcoran stands at the far left. While Captain Meagher stands on the other side of the cannon, facing the camera. (Dick Johnson Collection)

Officers and color party of the 53rd New York. This photo was probably taken at the same time as the similar view of the officers of the 28th Massachusetts (MASS/MOLLUS/USAMHI)

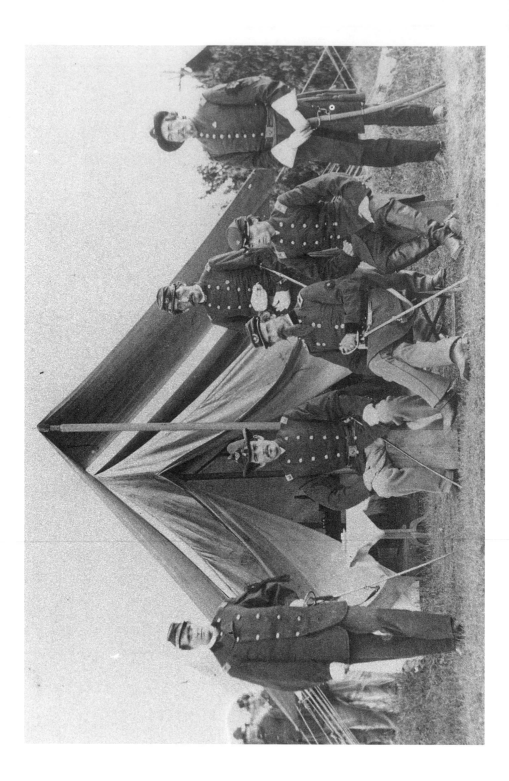

216

Commanding officers of the Irish Brigade in 1865. Standing, l. to r.: Major Seward F. Gould, 4th New York Heavy Artillery; Lieutenant Colonel James J. Smith, 69th New York; Major W. H. Terwilliger, 63rd New York. Seated, l. to r.: Colonel Denis F. Burke, 88th New York; Brevet Brigadier General Robert Nugent, Irish Brigade; Lieutenant Colonel James Flemming, 28th Massachusetts. When presented with the horse "Antietam" by his enlisted men, Lieutenant Colonel Burke, born in Cork, proudly declaimed that it was his "proudest boast that I commanded the 88th from Gettysburg to Petersburg." Lieutenant Colonel Smith presented Irish Brigade colors to the 69th New York National Guard on October 13, 1906. On that emotional occasion he let his "thoughts wander back to the remembrance of my loved, dead companions of the old Regiment and Brigade." (MASS/MOLLUS, USAMHI) Names of individuals from copy of picture in the Huntington Library.

218

Officers of the 28th Massachusetts. This photograph was probably taken close to or shortly after the end of the war. Standing, l. to r.: First Lieutenant Michael E. Powderly, First Lieutenant Thomas Cook, First Lieutenant John Knight, Mr. McParland, "citizen," Second Lieutenant George W. Beattie, First Lieutenant John Miner, Second Lieutenant William H. McCarthy, Assistant Surgeon Albert S. Chase, Second Lieutenant John McGlim. Seated, l. to r.: Captain John Miles, Captain Patrick W. Black, Lieutenant Colonel James Flemming, Captain Patrick H. Bird, Captain John Coriness. (MASS/ MOLLUS/USAMHI) Identifications, which differ slightly from those attached to the MASS/MOLLUS copy, are taken from another copy of this photograph in the Huntington Library collection.

Members of Companies A (Reenactment) and D (North-South Skirmish Association), 69th New York. L. to r. standing, Steve Garratano, Mike Bergman, Ron McGovern, Nick Ehlert, James Madden, Maurice A. "Bud" Scully. Kneeling l. to r., Neil Scully, Andy Megill, Steve Heist, Brian Scully. (Tony Hampton)

Officers and colors of the 69th New York Volunteers. This photograph probably dates from the end of the war, at the time of the Army of the Potomac's Grand Review (Library of Congress)

Strong circumstantial evidence suggests that the men in this photograph are members of Company F, 69th New York, and the image probably dates from June of 1865.

The soldier second from the right on the ground holds a forage cap with "F" and "69" on it. Only five states, Indiana, Illinois, Ohio, Pennsylvania and New York, fielded 69th regiments. These men have the look of eastern soldiers and only the New York and Pennsylvania regiments served in the eastern theater. The name "Moroney" is written in pencil on the reverse of the picture. No one by that name served in the 69th Pennsylvania's Company F, but Major Richard Moroney (aka Maroney)of the 69th New York initially served as a first lieutenant in the regiment's Company F.

The fact that the soldiers in the picture appear to have new, clean uniforms and tentage and NCO swords are on display indicates that their unit was in camp and perhaps awaiting a review. The tent styles are late war and there is foliage on the trees. As evidenced by several group photos of officers, there was a photographer in the Irish Brigade camp at the end of the war, perhaps at the time of the Grand Review of the Army of the Potomac. It is quite possible he took this picture as well. (Tom Molocea Collection)

The 69th remembers its own. Perhaps the most tradition conscious unit in the history of the United States army, the 69th New York sent a delegation to Ireland to commemorate the heroism of the regiment's Captain Patrick F. Clooney, killed in action at Antietam, September 17, 1862. One hundred years after Clooney's death, four members of the 69th (l. to r.) Private Patrick Heron, Private John O'Connor, Private First Class William Brennan and Private First Class Christopher Jones laid a wreath in honor of Clooney at his memorial stone in Ballybricken Church Yard, Waterford. (Lt. Col. Kenneth H. Powers Collection)

Color Guard composed of members of 69th New York Company A (reenactment) and D, (North-South Skirmish Association) October 8, 1994. L. to r., James Madden, Maurice A. "Bud" Scully Jr., Nicholas Ehlert, Charles Matthews. (Joseph Bilby)

The first flag of the 28th Massachusetts. Woodcut in *The Pilot*, January 18, 1862.

Officers and colors of the 63rd New York. The stacked muskets in the center are U. S. Model 1842s, which may be photographer's props. If not, they would date the picture as prior to the late summer of 1864, when the men of the 63rd turned in their smoothbores for rifle muskets. (John A. O'Brien/Irish American Cultural Society)

228

The restored "Prince of Wales Color" presented to the 69th Militia following Colonel Corcoran's snub of the heir to the British throne. (Veteran Corps, 69th New York)

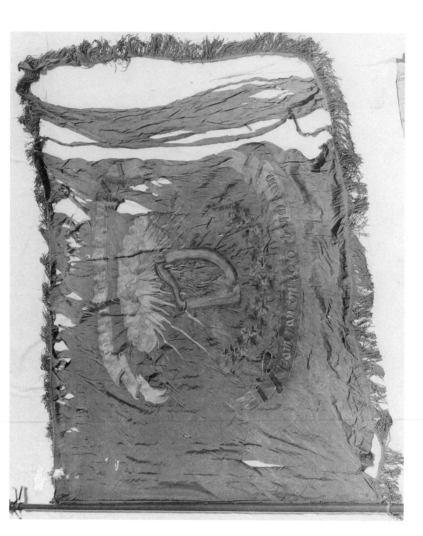

Remains of the first Irish flag of the 69th New York Volunteers. This flag was carried through the Peninsula campaign and at Antietam and also served, on loan from the 69th, on the *U. S. S. Antietam*. (U.S. Navy photo, Lt. Col. Kenneth H. Powers)

Members of Companies A (reenactors) and D, (North-South Skirmish Association) 69th New York. Silk flags are exact reproductions of the original embroidered colors of the original regiment. L. to R.: standing: Steve Garratano, Mike Bergman, Nick Ehlert, Ron McGovern, Jim Madden, Bud Scully; kneeling: Steve Heist, Andy Megill, Neil Scully, Brian Scully. (Ron DaSilva)

Second Irish Color, 69th New York. One of the flags presented to the New York regiments following Fredericksburg. This flag was restored and presented to the citizens of Ireland by President John F. Kennedy in 1963. It now hangs in the Irish Parliament building, Leinster House. (Lt. Col. Kenneth H. Powers Collection)

President John F. Kennedy presenting the 69th New York's restored second color to the Irish people in a ceremony held in the Dail in June of 1963. (Lt. Col. Kenneth H. Powers Collection)

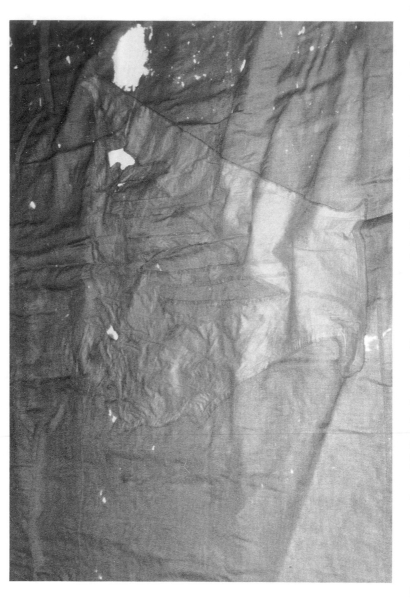

Cotton flag or camp color with battle damage. Recent research indicates this flag may have been carried by the 69th New York at Gettysburg. (Veteran Corps, 69th New York)

Remains of the first Irish flag of the 88th New York. (Veteran Corps, 69th New York)

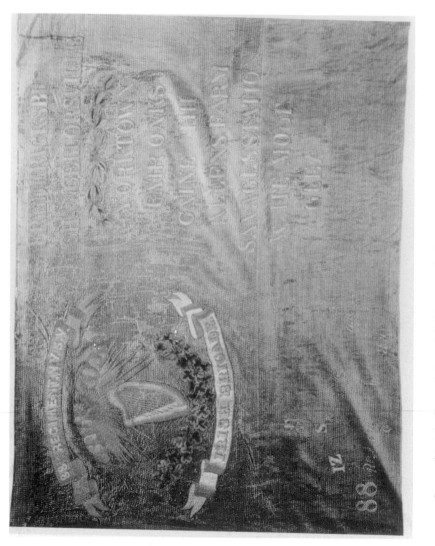

Second Irish flag of the 88th New York. (Veteran Corps, 69th New York)

A first sergeant of the 88th New York, with what appears to be a "camp color" or guidon. (Michael J. McAfee Collection)

The war torn flag of the 116th Pennsylvania (Lt. Col. Kenneth H. Powers collection)

NOTES

In order to avoid clutter, notes have been restricted to those identifying the sources of direct quotes and information which, while pertinent, would be out of place in the text. Citations have been abbreviated. For full titles of sources, please see the bibliography.

Notes to Introduction

1. Meagher is pronounced "Marr."
2. Fox, *Regimental Losses*, p. 118; Taylor, *Second Army Corps*, p. 5. According to Veteran Corps, 69th New York Commander Bernard Kelly, total brigade enrollment over the course of the war was 7,715.

Chapter One

1. Cavanagh, *Meagher*, p. 353-354.
2. Michael Corcoran to W. B. Field Esq., October 6, 1860, Lt. Col. Kenneth H. Powers collection.
3. *Harper's Weekly*, October 20, 1860, p. 658.
4. Conyngham, *Irish Brigade*, p. 21. Bernard Kelly notes an ironic twist in the history of the 69th's relationship with the British royal family. In 1944 King George VI awarded the regiment's commander, Colonel Gerard Kelley, the Distinguished Service Order for the 1943 recapture of Makin Atoll, a British protectorate, from the Japanese. Kelly, "Historic Civil War Colors." For more on the Irish "Wild Geese" in the French and other armies, see Appendix II.
5. *Irish American*, August 17, 1861.
6. *The Pilot*, August 10, 1861. From *The Pilot's* serialization of Thomas Meagher's *The Last Days of the 69th In Virginia*. Meagher's account was published by both the *Irish American* and *The Pilot* and later in pamphlet form. The work, extolling the virtues of the Irish soldier, helped Meagher lay the groundwork for recruiting his brigade.
7. *Last Days of the 69th*, *The Pilot*, August 10, 1861. A "buck and ball" cartridge for a muzzle loading .69 caliber smoothbore musket, with which the men of the 69th, excepting Company K, were armed, contained one .64 diameter round ball and three buckshot. The multi-projectile round increased a shooter's chances of hitting an enemy soldier with the inherently inaccurate smoothbore. Company K's Zouaves shouldered rifled .69 caliber muskets, which fired the more accurate conical minie ball. For more on small arms, see Appendix III.
8. Corcoran detailed the events of his capture in a letter published in the *The Pilot* on August 24, 1861; James McKay Rorty to Patrick Phelan, October 12,

239

1861, quoted in Brian C. Pohanka, "James McKay Rorty: An Appreciation" [n.p.] 1993, p. 6.

9. *Irish American*, August 17, 1861. After returning to New York the officers of the 69th expressed the regiment's "true and lasting gratitude" to Wildey. *The Pilot*, August 24, 1861.

10. *New York Commercial*, July 27, 1861, reprinted in *The Pilot*, August 3, 1861. The "stolen by Floyd" inference is most likely a reference to Former Secretary of War John B. Floyd, (1806-1863) who was accused of transferring U.S. military property including, in this case, a high crowned regulation army "Hardee hat," to seceding southern states in the waning days of the Buchanan administration. Floyd subsequently had a brief but undistinguished career as a Confederate brigadier general, dying of exposure rather than in battle.

11. *Ibid.*

12. The current 69th Regiment carries the battle honors of the 69th New York Militia, the 69th New York Volunteers and the 69th New York National Guard Artillery (182nd New York Volunteer Infantry) because the latter two units were provided with cadre personnel by the 69th Militia. As the sole surviving active regiment of the Irish Brigade, the current 69th is the custodian of the traditions of all the Irish Brigade regiments. *Army Lineage Book-Infantry*, pp. 477-499.

During the Civil War the New York Militia was renamed the National Guard, State of New York (NGSNY) and the 69th Militia became the 69th NGSNY. The regiment was again called to active duty on May 19, 1898, during the Spanish American War, but was still in a southern training camp when hostilities ceased.

The 69th entered Federal Service again during the Mexican Border Campaign of 1916 and, in World War I, was assigned to the famed 42nd "Rainbow Division," an outfit composed of elite National Guard regiments. Although the Federal government renumbered the 69th the 165th U.S. Infantry, the regiment was still the "Fighting 69th" to its men. The 69th found fame, glory and heavy casualties in Lorraine, Champagne-Marne, Aisne-Marne, St. Mihiel and the Meuse-Argonne. The regiment's most notable feat was forcing a crossing of the Ourcq River against a Prussian Guard division. The famed poet Joyce Kilmer, a sergeant in the 69th, was killed at the Ourcq.

Called to the colors again in 1940, the 69th, still the 165th Infantry to the army, fought in the Pacific theater in World War II. The regiment battled the Japanese on Makin Island, Saipan and Okinawa, where Company F won a Distinguished Unit Citation. A Medal of Honor awarded to a member of the regiment raised the unit's total to seven, (three in the Civil War and three in World War I) which may be the highest number earned by the soldiers of any National guard outfit.

In 1963 the 69th regained its number and was once again designated the 69th Infantry. In September 1993 the regiment became the 69th Air Defense Artillery (ADA). Perhaps more conscious of its traditions than any other U.S. army outfit, active, National Guard or reserve, the 69th acts as Military Escort for the Irish societies in the New York St. Patrick's Day Parade every March 17, which is, appropriately enough, formally designated "Regimental Day."

13. *Irish American*, September 14, 1861.

14. *New Jersey Herald*, (Newton) September 28, 1861.

15. *Irish American*, December 7, 1861. The folds of the flag hung heavy with Irish symbolism; the harp of Brian Boru, the legendary king who defeated the Vikings (and their Leinster allies) and met his death at Clontarf in 1014, the shamrocks with which St. Patrick explained the Trinity and converted Ireland, the sunburst which, to the Fenians, symbolized their links to ancient Ireland, and the recollection of the bard Oisin that his father, the famed warrior Fionn Mac Cumhal, and his spear, Mac an Loin " ...never retreated from the clash of spears," even when storming the gates of hell. Kelly, "Historic Civil War Colors."

16. Conyngham, *Irish Brigade*, p. 63.

17. Quoted in O'Flaherty, *69th New York*, p. 28.

18. *Irish American*, December 20, 21, 1861. Lieutenant James B. Turner of the 88th New York served on the brigade staff and was a regular correspondent of the *Irish American*, writing under the pen name "Gallowglass." Gallowglass, also spelled "galloglas," comes from the Irish "gall oglach" or "foreign warrior." The original gallowglass were professional soldiers who emigrated to Ireland from the Scottish Isles beginning in the 13th century. Local Irish lords eagerly hired these tough Scots of Norse/Celtic descent, who, in turn, recruited some native Irish into their ranks. Redoubtable warriors, the gallowglass relied on the axe as their primary weapon, and displayed a talent for organization and tactics unusual for the age. They failed to evolve, however, and lack of flexibility and the introduction of firearms eventually proved their undoing.

Turner was wounded at Antietam, promoted to captain and assigned to detached duty in New York. He rejoined the brigade staff in the spring of 1864 and was killed in action in the battle of the Wilderness.

19. *Irish American*, February 15, 1862.

20. O'Flaherty, *69th New York*. For a detailed look at Enright and his problems, see O'Flaherty.

21. *Irish American*, February 15, 1862.

22. *Ibid*, February 1, 1862.

23. Conyngham, *Irish Brigade*, pps. 560, 559; *Irish American*, February 1, 1862; *Irish Brigade*, p. 555.

24.   NY SARA, *For the Record*, Fall, 1989, p. 6.
25.   Peter Welsh to Patrick Prendergast, June 1, 1863, *Irish Green & Union Blue*, p. 103; Welsh to wife, February 3, 1863, Ibid, p. 65.
26.   Quoted in Miller, *Emigrants and Exiles*, p.359.
27.   James McKay Rorty to father, in Pohanka, "James McKay Rorty," p. 20-21.

Chapter Two

1.   Rafferty, "Experience of a private soldier."
2.   For a detailed account of buck and ball and smoothbore muskets in the Civil War, see Joseph G. Bilby, "A Better Chance ter Hit—the Story of Buck and Ball."
3.   W. L. D. O'Grady, "88th Regiment Infantry," in *New York at Gettysburg*, p. 516. "Big Mary" is most likely the woman who cooked for the 88th's Colonel Patrick Kelly and whom Peter Welsh mentioned was "sent to a prison in Washington" for smuggling liquor and selling it to enlisted men in late 1863. According to Welsh, Colonel Kelly's horse handler, who was probably Mrs. Gordon's husband, was court martialed for the same offense. A search of court martial records on file in the National Archives revealed no evidence of a court martial of a soldier named Gordon of the 88th, however. Welsh to wife, October 7, 1863, *Irish Green & Union Blue*. p. 128.
4.   *Irish American*, April 19, 1862.
5.   John Dwyer, "63rd Regiment," *New York at Gettysburg*, p. 493.
6.   Corby, *Chaplain Life*, p. 61.
7.   *OR*, Ser. I, Vol. XI, Pt. I, p. 776; Corby, *Chaplain Life*, p. 61
        Southern Virginia was home to a large number of poisonous snakes. The major of the 29th Massachusetts, which joined the Irish Brigade after Fair Oaks, informed his wife that his regiment was camped "just on the Border of the Dismal Swamp a miserable place. There are a great many of these Moccasin Snakes here. I saw one yesterday and another today. Jo Farmer of Co. D killed 2 today. Their bite is very poisonous." Charles Chipman to Dear Lissie, May 22, 1862, Charles Chipman Papers, USAMHI.
8.   Lyons, *Life of General Meagher*, p. 139.
9.   *OR*, Ser. I, Vol. XI, Pt. I, p. 777.
10.   Jersey City *Daily Courier and Advertiser*, June 13, 1862; O'Grady, "88th Regiment," p. 511. Although the identity of the correspondent of the *Daily Courier and Advertiser* is not identified, he may have been Lieutenant William M. McClelland of Jersey City, who was killed in action at Gettysburg and is buried in grave F-93, New York Plot, at Gettysburg National Cemetery. John M. Busey, *These Honored Dead*, p. 135
11.   Rafferty, "Experiences of a private soldier."

12. *Ibid.* The "will o' the wisp," often seen hovering above Irish marshes and boglands, where it was considered a spirit manifestation, would have been familiar to country Irishmen. To young Rafferty, raised in New York City, it would have been an eerie novelty.

13. Conyngham, *Irish Brigade*, p. 165.

14. Charles Chipman to "Dear Lissie," June 12, 1862, Chipman Papers, USAMHI.

15. *OR*, Ser. I, Vol. XI, Pt. II, p. 70.

16. *Ibid*, p. 70-71.

17. Beyer & Keydel, *Deeds of Valor*, p. 54.

18. *OR*, Ser. I, Vol. XI, Pt. II, p. 230.

19. *Irish American*, August 2, 1862.

20. O'Grady, "88th Regiment," p. 511.

21. Rafferty, "Experience of a private soldier."

22. Beyer & Keydel, *Deeds of Valor*, p. 60.

23. Badly disabled, Rafferty was discharged on March 5, 1863. He subsequently secured government employment in Washington, D.C. When Major General Jubal Early's 1864 raid approached the city limits, Rafferty was commissioned a 2nd lieutenant in the 6th D.C. Volunteers for the emergency. Happy to get into a fight once again, he fired "twenty rounds at them [the Rebels] at very close range on their flank, which ended my career as a soldier for Uncle Sam." Rafferty, "Experience of a private soldier."

Chapter Three

1. William L. D. O'Grady to editor of the *New York Herald*, February 10, 1917, *New York Herald*, February 12, 1917. Reprint of letter in Lt. Col. Kenneth H. Powers collection.

    O'Grady concluded: "Lincoln was not gushy, but the roll of the buck and ball muskets of the Brigade at Fair Oaks and their conduct on the seven days 'change of base' were matters of recent occurrence, and official commendation."

2. *Irish American*, August 2, 1862.

3. Quoted in O'Flaherty, *69th New York*, p. 138. A benefactor who identified himself only as "K," and who felt Meagher's oratory "strikes the nail on the head," started the bounty ball rolling with a contribution of $20 and a promise of $80 more. *Irish American*, August 2, 1862.

4. Quoted in O'Flaherty, *69th New York*, p. 151.

5. *Irish American*, September 27, 1862.

6. Edmund Halsey Diary, September 3, 1862, USAMHI; Dayton Flint to father, September 4, 1862, John Kuhl collection.

7. O'Grady, "88th Regiment," p. 512.

8.   *Irish American*, September 27, 1862.
9.   Beyer & Keydel, *Deeds of Valor*, p. 54.
10.   Conyngham, *Irish Brigade*, p. 405.
11.   One resident historian at Antietam National Battlefield Park believed the 69th and 88th may have been within ten yards of the Rebels at one point. Robert L. Lagemann to General Charles G. Stevenson, October 17, 1962. Lt. Col. Kenneth H. Powers collection.
12.   *Irish American*, October 25, 1862.
13.   *Irish American*, October 18, 1862; Conyngham, *Irish Brigade*, p. 551.
14.   Charles Chipman to "Dear Lissie,' September 25, 1862, Chipman Papers, USAMHI.

Both then and now, Meagher has been accused of deriving his courage from a bottle, which allegedly contributed to his fall. If truth be told, probably most Civil War officers went into combat with a flask close at hand. Interestingly, one American born Protestant Yankee wished "every man was like Thomas Francis Meagher in the army." R. G. Carter, *Four Brothers in Blue*, p. 183.

15.   In the late 1980s the remains of several Irish Brigade soldiers were discovered buried in a field near the Bloody Lane, some distance behind where the brigade's firing line was at the time of the battle. These men apparently died from small arms fire. They were killed either by Rebel skirmishers deployed far in front of the road during the brigade's initial advance or in the brief fight with Posey's Mississippians. The remains may also indicate the location of the brigade's field hospital, where a number of men died and were temporarily interred. The Alexander Gardner photograph of Irish Brigade dead at Antietam may depict some of these soldiers. The premise advanced in one account, that the men were killed by long range rifle musket fire from the Sunken Road to which the brigade, with its smoothbores, could not reply, is unlikely.

16.   Robert L. Lagemann to General Charles G. Stevenson, October 12, 1962, Lt. Col. Kenneth H. Powers collection; *Irish American*, October 11, 1862. Clooney's fellow soldiers raised money to have the captain, who had no relatives in America, reinterred in Calvary Cemetery in New York.

Several months after his death, a commemorative stone was erected in the young officer's memory in his native Waterford's Ballybricken Church Yard. The four sided monument was engraved, in part, thusly: "To the memory of Captain Patrick J. Clooney of the Pope's Irish Brigade and subsequently of Meagher's Irish American Brigade who fell gallantly leading his company at the Battle of Antietam, September 17, 1862, aged 21 years. Requiescat in pace."

The men of the 69th New York have a long memory for their own. On September 16, 1962, four uniformed members of the regiment laid a wreath at Clooney's Waterford memorial.

17. *Irish American*, November 22, 1862.

18. St. Clair Mulholland, *116th Pennsylvania*, p. 33.

19. Quoted in O'Flaherty, *69th New York*, p. 181; Walker, *Second Army Corps*, p. 136.

20. Headley, *Massachusetts in the Rebellion*, pp. 326-327. The flag intended for the 29th was eventually issued to another Massachusetts outfit, the solidly Irish 9th regiment.

21. Welsh to wife, November 30, 1862, *Irish Green & Union Blue*, p. 33. Byrnes had his work cut out for him when he was promoted from lieutenant in the 5th U.S. Cavalry to colonel in command of the 28th in October of 1862. The regiment's original colonel and lieutenant colonel had resigned under a cloud, and the outfit had slipped into a poor state of discipline and administrative disarray. Byrnes' regular army experience held him in good stead, however, and, despite a good deal of complaining, he soon had the 28th, a unit with excellent raw material, operating with the efficiency expected of an Irish Brigade regiment.

     Colonel Byrnes was familiar with many of the high and mighty in both Union and Confederate armies from his long regular army service as an enlisted man in the 1st U.S. Dragoons and 1st U.S. Cavalry. At one time, General "Jeb" Stuart was his company commander!

22. It is one of these "second issue" Irish Brigade flags, presented to the 69th, that is currently on display at Leinster House, the Republic of Ireland's parliament building. The 63rd's second color is at the University of Notre Dame and the 88th's resides in the 69th Regiment armory. It has been argued that these flags were not carried in combat, as surviving specimens show little battle damage. They do, however, appear with regimental groups in several photographs taken at the end of the war. For more details, see Kelly, "Historic Civil War Flags."

23. *Irish American*, January 3, 1863.

24. Walker, *Second Army Corps*, p. 153.

25. *Ibid*, P. 153-154.

26. Robert Nugent, "The Irish Brigade," *New York at Gettysburg*, p. 489. Cross was killed at Gettysburg.

27. William Miller Owen, "A Hot Day on Marye's Heights," *Battles and Leaders*, vol. III, p. 98.

28. Bismuth Miller, "Fredericksburg's Dead Line," Lt. Col. Kenneth H. Powers collection; Dwyer, "63rd Regiment," p. 500.

29. Nugent, "Irish Brigade," p. 489.

30. Corby, *Chaplain Life*, p. 132-133.

31. *Irish American*, January 3, 1863; Dwyer, "63rd Regiment," p. 500.

32. Miller, "Fredericksburg's Dead Line," Lt. Col. Kenneth H. Powers collection.

33.   O'Grady, "88th Regiment," p. 514.

34.   Miller, "Fredericksburg's Dead Line," Lt. Col. Kenneth H. Powers collection.

35.   Corby, *Chaplain Life*, p. 133.

36.   *Irish American*, January 3, 1863.

37.   Estimates of strengths and casualty figures vary. The II Corps historian stated
        that the 69th took 238 men into action and lost 128. Figures for the other
        regiments are: 88th, 252 and127; 63rd, 162 and 44; 28th, 416 and 158; 116th,
        247 and 88. Casualties include killed, wounded and missing. Walker, *Second
        Army Corps*, p. 192.

38.   O'Grady, "88th Regiment," p. 514; Corby, *Chaplain Life*, p. 135.

39.   Quoted in *The Pilot*, February 7, 1863.

40.   Conyngham, *Irish Brigade*, p. 350, 347; *Irish American*, January 10, 1863.

41.   *Irish American*, January 10, 1863. An officer of the 63rd recalled years after-
        ward, however, that after Meagher's speech concluded, "several round shot
        struck" the building, and "in short order the place was deserted." Dwyer, "63rd
        regiment," p. 500.

        This incident may have given birth to what would become the 69th New
        York's "Regimental Cocktail." Despatched to find "vise" [Vichy or seltzer]
        water to mix with whiskey, General Meagher's staff reportedly returned with
        champagne. The general mixed the two into a satisfying punch, which has
        survived down the years in the ranks of the 69th New York's Veteran Corps.
        It has also been sipped at Civil War reenactments and North-South Skirmish
        Association skirmishes. O'Flaherty, however, dates the creation of the drink,
        also known as the "Sixty-ninth or Meagher Cocktail," to the winter of 1861-
        1862 at Camp California. O'Flaherty, *69th New York*, p. 69.

42.   Conyngham, *Irish Brigade*, p. 359.

Chapter Four

1.   Peter Welsh to wife, January 4, 1863, *Irish Green and Union Blue*, p. 52; Joseph
        E. Sheedy to parents, January 20, 1863, Sheedy Pension File, NA. Quoted in
        Barry L. Spink, "From Cavan to Cold Harbor," p. 21.

2.   Fenianism and virulent anti-British sentiment may have been purely public
        posturing for at least some Irish Brigade officers. One historian has found a
        "striking contrast" between the private correspondence of James Turner and
        the fervid Irish nationalism expressed in his "Gallowglass" letters in the *Irish
        American*. William L. Burton, *Melting Pot Soldiers*, pp. 121-122.

3.   Thomas Francis Galwey, *The Valiant Hours*, p. 74; Pohanka, "Rorty Apprecia-
        tion," p. 12.

4.   Galwey, *The Valiant Hours*, p. 75.

5.   Conyngham, *Irish Brigade*, p. 367. "Pioneers," were men detailed from the in-

fantry to build field fortifications, clear roads on the march and cut their way through the "abatis" of downed trees guarding the approaches to enemy fortifications. In today's army they would be referred to as "combat engineers."

At any given time, 10% to 15% of a Civil War infantry regiment's strength was on detail. A lack of developed support and combat support branches led to these assignments, which weakened infantry outfits. Examples of such details include military police, blacksmiths, small arms ordnance men, quartermaster clerks and wagon and ambulance drivers. Some men on permanent detail never actually served with their regiments, although they were carried on the rolls and discharged with them at the end of the war.

6. Corby, *Chaplain Life*, p. 101.
7. Conyngham, *Irish Brigade*, pp. 374, 376.
8. *Ibid*, p. 373.
9. Corby, *Chaplain Life*, p. 28. The "Father Matthew" temperance movement was founded by Father Theobald Matthew, whose memorial statue stands in the center island of Dublin's O'Connell Street. Most Dubliners seem unaware of this, however, and the author was advised by a native of the city that he could win a bet on the statue's identity in any Dublin pub.
10. Mulholland, *116th Regiment*, p. 90. Corps badges were assigned to the Army of the Potomac thusly: I Corps, circle; II Corps, trefoil; III Corps, diamond; V Corps, Maltese cross; VI Corps, Greek or Saint Andrew's cross; XI Corps, crescent; XII Corps, star.

    It has been said that the "trefoil" is, in fact a shamrock and was selected because of the large number of Irish troops in the II Corps. If that was not originally the case, it certainly came to be. The 69th ADA, lineal descendent of the 69th New York Militia, the 69th New York Infantry and the 69th New York Heavy Artillery, proudly carries the red "shamrock" of the II Corps' First Division on its unit crest to this day.

    By 1863, most Federal corps had three divisions. Insignia for first divisions was red, second divisions, white and third divisions, blue. If a corps had a fourth division, as happened occasionally, that unit's badge would be green.
11. Hiram T. Nason to W. W. Sanborn, May 2, 1863, Nason Pension File, NA. Quoted in Barry L. Spink, "From Cavan to Cold Harbor," p. 25.
12. Mulholland, *116th Pennsylvania*, p. 109.
13. *Ibid*, p. 110.
14. O'Grady, "88th Regiment," p. 515. John W. Busey and David Martin, in *Regimental Strengths at Gettysburg*, p. 36, give the brigade strength at 700, with 532 men actually engaged. Busey and Martin's engaged figures for the brigade are: Field & Staff, 2; 28th Massachusetts, 224; 63rd New York, 75; 69th New York, 75; 88th New York, 90; 116th Pennsylvania, 66.

Chapter Four

15. Corby, *Chaplain Life*, p. 184. Corby was not the first or only priest to absolve the brigade before battle. At White Oak Swamp on the Peninsula, Father Dillon of the 63rd said: "let every soldier, officer and private, catholic and Non-Catholic, fall on his knees, and repeat with me a sincere act of contrition for their past sins, after which I will impart absolution in the name of Christ." Dwyer, "63rd Regiment," p. 498. Fathers Corby and Ouellet blessed the battle line going into the fight at Antietam.
16. Mulholland, *116th Pennsylvania*, p. 137.
17. *OR*, Ser. I, Vol. XXVII, Pt. I, P. 380.
18. Although the sacrifice of General Caldwell's division gained precious time for the Union in the early evening hours of July 2, 1863, an unforgiving General Hancock apparently held Caldwell responsible for badly handling and wrecking his old command. When the Army of the Potomac was reorganized in the spring of 1864, Caldwell found himself without a job. He spent the rest of the war on staff assignments in Washington.
19. *Irish American*, August 1, 1863.
20. Welsh to wife, July 17, 1863, *Irish Green & Union Blue*, p. 110; Welsh to wife, August 2, 1863, *Ibid*, p. 115.
21. Mulholland, *116th Pennsylvania*, p. 164.
22. *Ibid*, p. 165.

Chapter Five

1. Conyngham, *The Irish Brigade*, p. 433-436.
2. *The Pilot*, May 30, 1863. Corcoran died shortly after conferring with Thomas F. Meagher, who visited his brigade's camp in Virginia. The men separated on a friendly basis and Meagher left Corcoran his horse, which the general was riding at the time of his death. It is generally believed that Corcoran had a stroke, which caused him to fall from the horse.

    Although probably the most pro-war Fenian, even Corcoran occasionally expressed ambivalence on wholesale Irish enlistments, probably due to the fact that heavy casualties could wipe out the Fenian movement as well as Irish units.
3. *Irish American*, December 26, 1863.
4. O'Donovan Rossa to *Cork Examiner*, April 23, 1863, reprinted in *Irish American*, May 16, 1863. O'Donovan Rossa had an interest in who won the war. He had two brothers and a brother-in-law in the Union forces. On the other hand, John Mitchel, one of General Meagher's fellow "Young Irelanders," edited the *Richmond Enquirer* and had three sons in the Confederate army. Two of Mitchel's sons were killed in action and one lost an arm. Father John Bannon, who served as a Confederate chaplain in the early part of the war,

returned to Ireland and distributed anti-Union propoganda with a good deal of success. For a detailed analysis of Irish attitudes in Ireland towards the American Civil War, see Hernon, *Celts, Catholics & Copperheads.*

5. *Irish American*, March 15, 1864; *The Pilot*, March 19, 1864; John Connor to Thomas, Dublin Metropolitan Police Report, Registered State Papers, #16,765 (1864) National Archives, Republic of Ireland. This file contains a variety of reports, letters and documents on the Finney incident. Two of the unfortunate Irishmen who joined the 20th Maine were killed in action and several others wounded or disabled by disease before the survivors were discharged through the auspices of the British Consul.

6. Quoted in Miller, *Emmigrants and Exiles*, p. 361.

7. *Irish American*, April 19. 1864.

8. Headley, *Massachusetts in the Rebellion*, p. 322.

9. Corby, *Chaplain Life*, p. 232.

10. Quoted in Bates, *Pennsylvania Volunteers*, Vol. III, p. 1232. The cartridge for the .69 caliber smoothbore musket, like that for the .58 caliber rifle musket, was encased in paper. When loading a rifle musket, the soldier bit his cartridge open, poured the powder charge down his gun's barrel, threw away the paper, inserted the bullet in the barrel's muzzle and rammed it home before affixing a percussion cap to the nipple, or cone, under the hammer. the smoothbore armed soldier would also open his cartridge with his teeth, but then ram the whole round, buckshot, ball, powder and paper, down the barrel. Burning paper from fired buck and ball rounds set the 116th's works afire.

11. Reid Mss., Veteran Corps, 69th NY.

12. Mulholland, *116th Pennsylvania*, p. 198.

13. Dwyer, "63rd Regiment," p. 504.

14. Colonel Byrnes had survived severe gunshot and lance wounds suffered in frontier fights with Apaches in the 1850s while serving as an enlisted man. He left a widow and three children in Jersey City. For a detailed biography of Byrnes see Barry L. Spink, "From Cavan to Cold Harbor."

15. *OR*, Ser. I, Vol. XXXVI, Pt. I, pp. 390-391.

16. Mulholland, *116th Pennsylvania*, p. 229.

Chapter Six

1. Mulholland, *116th Pennsylvania*, p. 235.

2. *Irish American*, July 2, 1864.

3. Dwyer, "63rd Regiment," p. 505.

4. Mulholland, *116th Pennsylvania*, p. 247. Surviving ordnance records (see appendix) indicate that the 63rd, 69th, and 88th were also issued rifle muskets during the third quarter of 1864, ending the smoothbore era for the Irish

Brigade.

5. *The Pilot*, October, 1, 1864.
6. *Ibid.*
7. *OR*, Ser. I, Vol. XLII, Pt. III, p. 477.
8. *The Pilot*, October 1, 1864.
9. *OR*, Ser. I, Vol. XLII, Pt. I, p. 258.
10. Sergeant McGrath was promoted to first lieutenant with rank dating from November 8, 1864 and was exchanged on February 22, 1865. He remained in the regular army after the war and eventually retired in California, where he died in 1923. Although he was a fine soldier, McGrath's progeny would exceed his fame. He was the great grandfather of Thomas Clancy, a founder of the well known Irish singing group, The "Clancy Brothers." Service Records of Thomas McGrath, NA and correspondence with Thomas Clancy.
11. *Ibid*, p. 255.
12. *Irish American*, April 1, 1865.
13. *The Pilot*, April 1, 1865.
14. *Irish American*, April 1, 1864.
15. Headley, *Massachusetts in the Rebellion*, p. 325.
16. *Irish American*, July 15, 1865. Robert Nugent gives the brigade a strength of "less than a thousand" upon its arrival in New York in 1865. Nugent, "Irish Brigade," p. 490.
17. *Ibid.*

Epilogue

1. Corby, *Chaplain Life*, p.192.

Recessional

1. "Address delivered at the Armory of the 69th Regt., N.Y.N.G., Oct. 13, 1906, on the presentation of the Battle Flags of the Irish Brigade, by Col. James J. Smith, 69th Regt., N.Y. Vet. Vols." Typescript in Lt. Col. Kenneth H. Powers collection.

Appendix 1

1. D'Arcy, *Fenian Movement*, pps. 32, 26.
2. Quoted in Burton, *Melting Pot Soldiers*, p. 126.
3. *The Pilot*, August 17, 1861.
4. O'Grady, "88th Regiment," p. 513, "Experiences of a private soldier."
5. Quoted in Burton, *Melting Pot Soldiers*, p. 123.

6. David E. Sparks, ed., *Inside Lincoln's Army*, p. 414; Seward R. Osborne, ed., *The Civil War Diaries of Col. Theodore B. Gates*, p. 152.

7. Sparks, ed., *Inside Lincoln's Army*, p. 415.

8. Robert W. Daly, *Aboard the USS Monitor: 1862*, pp. 187-188.

9. Malone & Roeder, *Montana*, p. 77. For a concise history of Montana's convoluted politics in the early postwar period and Meagher's role in the state's history, see Malone & Roeder, pp. 76-82. For more detail, particularly on Meagher, see Robert G. Athearn, *Thomas Francis Meagher*.

10. Quoted in Frederick B. Arner, *The Mutiny at Brandy Station*, p. 165.

11. Robert G. Athearn, Meagher's most critical biographer, asserts that "there is as much evidence to show that he [Meagher] was ill rather than drunk," at the time of his death and that "the legend of his insobriety ... gave his enemies a chance to blacken his name." Athearn, *Meagher*, p. 166.

Appendix 3

1. O'Grady, "88th Regiment," p. 511

2. Willard, *Rifled and Smooth Bored Arms*, p. 13. Interestingly, when Willard was killed at Gettysburg commanding the Third Brigade of the Third Division of the Third Corps, all of his regiments, including the 125th New York, were armed with rifle muskets.

3. McAllister to wife, September 19, 1862, in Robertson, ed., *McAllister Letters*, p. 209.

"Honor to the Brave 69th." Souvenir card, probably dating from 1861 and commemorating the 69th Militia's fight at Bull Run. (Dick Johnson Collection)

BIBLIOGRAPHY
Books, Pamphlets and Published Documents

Alotta, Robert I. *Civil War Justice: Union Army Executions Under Lincoln.* Shippensburg, PA: White Mane, 1989.

Arner, Frederick B. *The Mutiny at Brandy Station: The Last Battle of the Hooker Brigade.* Kensington, MD: Bates & Blood Press, 1993.

Athearn, Robert G. *Thomas Francis Meagher: An Irish Revolutionary in America.* Boulder, CO: University of Colorado Press, 1949.

Bates, Samuel P. *History of Pennsylvania Volunteers, 1861-1865*, Vol III. Harrisburg PA: B. Singerly, 1870.

Beyer, W. F. & O. F. Keydal. *Deeds of Valor: How America's Civil War Heroes Won the Medal of Honor.* Detroit: Perrian-Keydal Co., 1903.

Bilby, Joseph G. *Three Rousing Cheers: A History of the Fifteenth New Jersey Infantry from Flemington to Appomattox.* Hightstown, NJ: Longstreet House, 1993.

Boatner, Mark M. III. *The Civil War Dictionary.* New York: David MacKay Company Inc., 1959.

Bredin, A. E. C. *A History of the Irish Soldier.* Belfast: Century Books, 1987.

Burton, William L. *Melting Pot Soldiers: the Union's Lithnic Regiments.* Iowa State University Press, 1988.

Busey, John W. and Dr. David G.Martin. *Regimental Strengths at Gettysburg.* Baltimore: Gateway Press, 1982.

Busey, John W. *These Honored Dead: The Union Casualties at Gettysburg.* Hightstown, NJ: Longstreet House, 1988.

Cannan, John. *The Wilderness Campaign: May, 1864.* Conshohocken, PA: Combined Books, 1993.

Carter, Robert Goldthwaite. *Four Brothers in Blue: Or Sunshine and Shadows of the War of the Rebellion. A Story of the Great Civil War from Bull Run to Appomattox.* Austin: University of Texas Press, 1978.

Conyngham, David P. *The Irish Brigade and its Campaigns*, New York: William McSorley & Co., 1866.

Corby, William, C.S.C. (Lawrence F. Kohl ed.) *Memoirs of Chaplain Life:*

Three Years With the Irish Brigade in the Army of the Potomac. New York: Fordham University Press, 1992.

Cooling, Benjamin Franklin and Walton H. Owen II. *Mr. Lincoln's Forts: A Guide to the Civil War Defenses of Washington.* Shippensburg, PA: White Mane, 1988.

Cunliffe, Marcus. *Soldiers & Civilians: The Martial Spirit in America.* New York: The Free Press, 1973.

Daly, Robert W., ed. *Aboard the Monitor: 1862; The Letters of Acting Paymaster William Frederick Keeler, U. S. Navy to His Wife, Anna.* Annapolis: U. S. Naval Institute, 1964.

D'Arcy, William O.F.M. Conv. *The Fenian Movement in the United States: 1858-1886.* Washington: Catholic University Press, 1947.

Dungan, Myles. *Distant Drums: Irish Soldiers in Foreign Armies.* Belfast: Appletree Press, 1993.

Fox, William F. *Regimental Losses in the American Civil War, 1861-1865.* Albany: Brandow Printing Company, 1898.

Frassanito, William A. *Antietam: The Photographic Legacy of America's Bloodiest Day.* New York: Charles Scribner's Sons, 1978.

Gallagher, Gary W., ed. *The Second Day at Gettysburg: Essays on Confederate and Union Leadership.* Kent, OH: Kent State University Press, 1994.

Griffith, Paddy. *Battle Tactics of the Civil War.* New Haven: Yale University Press, 1989.

Hayes-McCoy, Gerard A. *Irish Battles: A Military History of Ireland.* London: Longmans, Green & Co., Ltd., 1969.

_____. *The History of Irish Flags.* Dublin: Academy Press, 1979.

Headley, P. C. *Massachusetts in the Rebellion: A Record of the Historical Position of the Commonwealth and the Services of the Leading Statesmen, the Military, the Colleges, and the People, in the Civil War of 1861-1865.* Boston: Walker, Fuller, and Co., 1866.

Hernon, Joseph M. Jr. *Celts, Catholics & Copperheads: Ireland Views the American Civil War.* Columbus, OH: Ohio State University Press, 1968.

Johnson, Robert U. and Clarence C. Buel, eds. *Battles and Leaders of the Civil War.* New York: The Century Company, 1887.

Jones, Paul. *The Irish Brigade*. New York: Luce, 1969.

Jones, Terry I. *Lee's Tigers: The Louisiana Infantry in the Army of Northern Virginia*. Baton Rouge: LSU Press, 1987.

Kenny, Michael. *The Fenians: Photographs and Memorabilia from the National Museum of Ireland*. Dublin: Country House, 1994.

Kohl, Lawrence F. and Margaret Cosse Richard, eds. *Irish Green and Union Blue: The Civil War Letters of Peter Welsh*. New York: Fordham University Press, 1986.

Ladd, David L. and Audrey J. Ladd, eds. *The Bachelder Papers: Vol. I*. Dayton, OH: Morningside Press, 1994.

Lonn, Ella. *Foreignors in the Union Army and Navy*. Baton Rouge: LSU Press, 1951.

Lyons, W. F. *Brigadier General Thomas Francis Meagher: His Political and Military Career; With Selections from His Speeches and Writings*. New York: D. & J. Sadlier & Co., 1870.

Malone, Michael P. and Richard B. Roeder. *Montana: A History of Two Centuries*. Seattle: University of Washington Press, 1976.

Matter, William D. *If It Takes All Summer: The Battle of Spotsylvania*. Chapel Hill: UNC Press, 1988.

McLaughlin, Mark G. *The Wild Geese: The Irish Brigades of France and Spain*. London: Osprey, 1980.

Meagher, Thomas Francis. *The Last Days of the Sixty Ninth in Virginia*. New York: Irish American, 1861.

Menge, W. Springer and J. August Shimrak, eds. *The Civil War Notebook of Daniel Chisholm*. [116th PA] New York: Ballentine, 1989.

Miller, Kerby A. *Emigrants and Exiles: Ireland and the Irish Exodus to North America*. New York: Oxford University Press, 1985.

Moody, T. W. and F. X. Martin, eds. *The Course of Irish History*. New York: Weybright and Talley, 1967.

Mulholland, St. Clair A. *The Story of the 116th Regiment, Pennsylvania Infantry: War of Secession, 1862-1865*. Gaithersburg, MD: Old Soldier Books, 1992. [reprint]

New York Monuments Commission for the Battlefields of Gettysburg and Chattanooga. *Final Report on the Battlefield of Gettysburg*. [New York *at Gettysburg*] Three Vols. Albany: J. B. Lyon Co., 1900, 1902.

O'Faolain, Sean. *The Irish: A Character Study.* New York: Devin-Adair, 1956.

O'Flaherty, Very Rev. Patrick D. *History of the Sixty-Ninth Regiment in the Irish Brigade, 1861-1865.* Ann Arbor: University Microfilms, 1976.

Palfrey, F. W. *The Antietam and Fredericksburg.* New York: Charles Scribner's Sons, 1882.

Osborne, Seward, ed. *The Civil War Diaries of Col. Theodore B. Gates, 20th New York State Militia.* Hightstown, NJ: Longstreet House, 1991.

Pfanz, Harry W. *Gettysburg: The Second Day.* Chapel Hill NC: UNC Press, 1987.

Priest, John Michael. *Antietam: The Soldiers' Battle.* Shippensburg, PA: White Mane, 1989.

Robertson, James I., ed. *The Civil War Letters of General Robert McAllister.* New Brunswick, NJ: Rutgers University Press, 1965.

Sears, Stephen W. *To the Gates of Richmond: The Peninsula Campaign.* New York: Ticknor & Fields, 1992.

Sparks, David S., ed. *Inside Lincoln's Army: The Diary of Marsena Rudolph Patrick, Provost Marshal General, Army of the Potomac.* New York: Thomas Yoseloff, 1964.

Squier, E. G. ed. *Frank Leslie's Pictorial History of the American Civil War,* Vol I. New York: Frank Leslie, 1862.

Taylor, Frank H. *Philadelphia in the Civil War, 1861-1865.* Philadelphia: City of Philadelphia, 1913.

Trudeau, Noah Andre. *Bloody Roads South: The Wilderness to Cold Harbor, May-June, 1864.* New York: Ballentine, 1989.

U. S. War Department. *The War of the Rebellion: A Compilation of the Official Records of the Union and Confederate Armies.* 128 Vols. Washington, D. C.: U. S. Government Printing Office, 1880-1901.

Walker, Francis A. *History of the Second Army Corps.* New York: Charles Scribner's Sons, 1887.

White, Russell C., ed. *The Civil War Diary of Wyman S. White, First Sergeant, Company F, 2nd United States Sharpshooters.* Baltimore: Butternut and Blue Press, 1993.

Wilkinson, Warren. *Mother, May You Never See the Sights I Have Seen: The Fifty Seventh Massachusetts Veteran Volunteers in the Last Year of the Civil War.* Harper & Row, New York, 1990.

Willard, George L. *Comparative Value of Rifled and Smooth Bored Arms.* Washington [n. p.] 1863.

Articles

Bilby, Joseph G., "Remember Fontenoy: The 69th New York and the Irish Brigade in the American Civil War," *Military Images Magazine*, Vol. IV, No. 5, March-April, 1983.

_____, "A Better Chance Ter Hit -- The Story of Buck and Ball," *American Rifleman*, May, 1993.

Campbell, Eric, "Caldwell Takes the Wheatfield," *Gettysburg Magazine*, Issue Number Three, July, 1990.

Garland, J. L., "Some Notes on the Irish During the First Month of the American Civil War," *Irish Sword*, Vol. V, Summer, 1961.

Lang, Wendall W. Jr., "Corps Badges, Pt. I: First through Fifth Army Corps," *Military Images Magazine*, Vol. VII, No. 6, May-June, 1986.

Lonergan, Thomas H., "Thomas Francis Meagher," *American Irish Historical Society Journal*, Vol. XII, 1913.

Maryniak, Ben, "Their Faith Brings Them," *Civil War*, Vol. IX, No. 2, March-April, 1991.

McAfee, Michael, "69th Regiment, New York State Militia - The National Cadets - 1861,' *Military Images Magazine*, Vol. XI, No. 5, March-April, 1990.

McCormack, Jack, "A Touch of Green Among the Blue: Irish Troops in the Army of the Potomac," *Military Images Magazine*, Vol. XI, No. 5, March-April, 1990.

_____, "Blue, Gray and Green: The Fighting Irish," *Civil War*, Vol. IX, No. 2, March-April, 1991.

Miller, Bismuth, "Fredericksburg's Dead Line," *The Sun* [New York] April 22, 1911. (Copy in Lt. Col. Kenneth H. Powers Collection)

New York State Archives & Records Administration, "Irish Immigrants in the Civil War: Fighting for Acceptance," *For the Record*, Vol. VII,

#4. Fall, 1989.

Nugent, Robert, "General Nugent's Description of the Sixty-Ninth Regiment at Fredericksburg," *Third Annual Report of the State Historian of the State of New York*, 1897.

O'Brien, Kevin E., "Commands -- The Irish Brigade," *America's Civil War*, May, 1994.

Purcell, Richard J., "Ireland and the American Civil War," *Catholic World*, Vol. CXV, 1922.

Rogers, Stephen, "A Bridge Too Many -- Or, How to Be in Two Places at Once," *Military Images Magazine*, Vol. XIII, No. 4, January-February, 1992.

"Unmarked Graves Give a Glimpse Into a Civil War Soldier's Life," *New York Times*, September, 16, 1994.

Other Studies

Conconnan, John J., "Colorful and Gallant General Michael Corcoran." Monograph to accompany memorial ceremony at Calvary Cemetery, Queens, New York, April 29, 1990.

Culleton, Edward, "John Kavanaugh, Young Irelander, 1847-1862." Typescript in the John Kavanaugh Papers, United States Army Military History Institute, Carlisle, PA

Kelly, Bernard B., "The Chaplains of the 69th Regiment of New York." Monograph to accompany Irish Brigade Association Encampment, 1990.

———, "The Historic Civil War Irish Colors of the 69th Regiment." Unpublished Monograph, 1994.

Murphy, William A., "The Charge of the Irish Brigade at Marye's Heights in the Battle of Fredericksburg, Virginia During the American Civil War." Unpublished Monograph, 1965. Possession of Veteran Corps, 69th Regt. Inc..

Pohanka, Brian, "James McKay Rorty: A Worthy Officer, A Gallant Soldier, An Estimable Man." Monograph to accompany memorial ceremony at Calvary cemetery, Queens, New York, 1993.

McAfee, Michael J., "69th New York State Militia, Company K (Irish

Zouaves) 1861." Monograph to accompany Don Troiani print, 1988.

McLaughlin, James H., "James Haggerty of Tir Conaill, Irish Patriot -- American Hero." Monograph to accompany memorial ceremony at Calvary Cemetery, Queens, New York, 1992.

Noonan, J. "69th New York History." Typescript, Kenneth H. Powers Collection, United States Army Military History Institute.

O' Grady, William L. D., "Lincoln and the Irish Flag." Letter to *New York Herald*, February 10, 1917. Copy of reprint in Lt. Col. Kenneth H. Powers Collection.

Powers, Lt. Col. Kenneth H., "Raise the Colors and Follow Me: The Irish Brigade at the Battle of Antietam." Monograph to accompany Mort Kunstler print, n. d..

_____, "The Fighting 69th -- The Sixty-Ninth Regiment of New York, Its History, Heraldry, Tradition and Customs." Monograph to accompany the 1993 New York State Ancient Order of Hibernians Convention.

_____, "The Meagher Sword." Monograph detailing the history of the recovery of General Meagher's Sword n. d..

Smith, Col. James J., "Address delivered at the Armory of the 69th Regt. N. Y. N. G., Oct. 13, 1906, on the presentation of the Battle Flags of the Irish Brigade, by Col. James J. Smith, 69th Regt. N. Y. Vet. Vols.." Typescript in Lt. Col. Kenneth H. Powers collection.

Spink, Barry I., "From Cavan to Cold Harbor: The Life of Colonel Richard Byrnes." Monograph to accompany memorial ceremony at Calvary Cemetery, Queens, New York, 1994.

Newspapers

Irish American, New York

The Pilot, Boston

Jersey City *Courier*

New York *Times*

Manuscripts and Letters

Chipman, Charles, Letters. United States Army Military History Institute, Carlisle, PA. [29th Mass.]

Carman, Ezra A, Maps prepared for the Antietam Battlefield Board, Antietam National Battlefield Park. (Copies courtesy Lt. Col. Kenneth H. Powers)

Clancy, Thomas L. to author, August 23, 1994, with service and pension records of Thomas McGrath.

Corby, Rev. William, "Scene of a Religious Character on the Historic Battlefield of Gettysburg," Gettysburg National Military Park.

Corcoran, Michael, to W. B. Field, Esq., October 6, 1860. Lt. Col. Kenneth H. Powers collection.

Flint, Dayton. Letters copied and transcribed from Washington, NJ *Star.* John Kuhl collection.

Halsey, Edmund. Journal, United States Army Military History Institute, Carlisle, PA.

Holmes, Orrin D., Letters. Civil War Miscellaneous Collection, United States Army Military History Institute, Carlisle, PA. [29th Mass.]

Rafferty, Peter. "Experience of a private soldier during the Peninsula Campaign, 1862. Company B, 69th N. Y. Vol.." New York State Archives.

Reid, William F. "Report of the Irish Brigade While Under General U. S. Grant." Possession of Veteran Corps, 69th Regiment Inc. [28th Mass.]

Registered State Papers, 1864, #16,765. National Archives, Republic of Ireland.

GENERAL INDEX

GENERAL INDEX

GENERAL INDEX

GENERAL INDEX

264

GENERAL INDEX

GENERAL INDEX

GENERAL INDEX

GENERAL INDEX

GENERAL INDEX

AUTHOR BIOGRAPHY

Joseph G. Bilby was born in Newark, New Jersey. He received his B.A. and M.A. degrees from Seton Hall University and served as a lieutenant with the First Infantry Division in Vietnam in 1966-1967. Mr. Bilby is employed by the New Jersey Department of Labor and has taught military history at Ocean County College. He is the author of over 200 magazine articles on military and New Jersey history and outdoor subjects and is a contributing editor for *Military Images Magazine* and a columnist for *The Civil War News*. He is also the author of *Three Rousing Cheers: A History of the Fifteenth New Jersey Infantry from Flemington to Appomattox* and *Forgotten Warriors: New Jersey's African-American Civil War Soldiers*. Mr. Bilby is a member of the Outdoor Writers' Association of America, the Irish Brigade Association and the North-South Skirmish Association's 69th New York. He lives at the New Jersey shore with his wife, three children and labrador retriever.